THEOLOGY *of* HOME II

THEOLOGY *of* HOME II

THE SPIRITUAL ART *of* HOMEMAKING

CARRIE GRESS

NOELLE MERING

Photography by **KIM BAILE**

with Dori Greco Rutherford

TAN Books

ISBN: 978-1-5051-1700-4

Published in the United States by
TAN Books
PO Box 269
Gastonia, NC 28053
www.TANBooks.com

Printed in the United States of America

Contents

Authors' Note

Since the subject of home is so personal, it was only natural for us to include personal stories from our lives as wives and mothers. But as the nature of co-authorship dictates, you don't always know who is speaking. Part of the beauty of this book is the universal theme of home, and as such, our personal stories are meant to convey deeper truths, making the actual owner of our individual stories not nearly as important as the message the story conveys. We hope this does not distract from your reading of the text.

Introduction

Embracing Home, Rejecting Homemaking

Betty Friedan called it the "ache with no name."

It was a concept that resonated and reverberated in the West, hitting a nerve with 1960s women. Believing that this nameless ache was due to life at home, women fled in droves in search of more meaning, success, acclaim, and money beyond the four walls they believed enslaved them.

Six decades later, women are still plagued with a nameless ache—a desire for something they can't quite put their finger on. Friedan, had she known her faith tradition of Judaism, would have recognized this ache as a desire for God. Christians know this ache too. St. Augustine famously summarized it when he said, "Our hearts are made for you, O Lord, and they are restless until they rest in you." He was identifying the desire that all men and women have for the eternal, for something beyond the passing pleasures and delights this world offers.

For decades now, the entrenched wisdom has been that women's unhappiness is largely due to the fact that home life demeans us, and the remedy is for us to demean it in return. Overlooked has been the possibility that perhaps home had precious little to do with our ache in the first place. Since Friedan's declaration, we have looked high and low, but that ache is still there, as every happiness metric shows. Statistics on depression, suicide, substance abuse, and divorce point to the general reality that vast majorities of women are truly and deeply unhappy.

But the pendulum seems to be swinging in a different direction. Back toward home. Over the past decade, our culture has seen a resurgence of interest in the domestic arts. What was old seems new again. Contemporary McMansions are shunned for old farmhouses or low-slung mid-century homes. Convenience food is now something we buy sheepishly, opting instead to wear aprons while making simple, slow meals served on hand-thrown pottery. We knit, sew, quilt, and even quill. If it is a craft, it has probably made, or is about to make, a social comeback from relative obscurity.

What is interesting about this rise in the domestic arts is that it is not necessarily springing from an equal rise in our appreciation of homemaking. There continues to be a disconnect between loving our homes and recognizing the important and real value of a homemaker. While we can interpret this in different ways, there seems to be a general consensus that we like the trappings of what homemakers do without the actual daily grind of making a home for others. Why? Much of this stems from the irrational social taboos against homemaking ignited by Betty Friedan and others, but the answer is more complex.

If we look to various metrics to understand how humans define happiness, a few patterns emerge. While lists vary, bestselling author and consultant Patrick Lencioni discusses three common elements to evaluate career happiness. Lencioni asks:

1. Am I respected and known in my job?
2. Do I know why my job matters?
3. Am I progressing in my work, and is there a measure for this progress?

If the answer to any of these is no, an individual may feel disillusioned in her current role. What happens when we apply these questions to homemakers?

"Am I respected and known in my job?" is not a box that many homemakers would check. While there are exceptions and wonderful communities to be found in support of homemakers, one doesn't have to look far to feel the chill sweeping in from the broader culture.

Even a quick trip to the neighborhood Trader Joe's is revelatory. While the employees are always friendly, the customer base often is not. Sighs, eye rolls, and veiled remarks are all things a mom with a crew of little people may have to contend with in one of America's smallest grocery store chains. Too often, what is wordlessly communicated is that the mother with children stands in the way of the very important professional's day.

"The first supermarket supposedly appeared on the American landscape in 1946. That is not very long ago. Until then, where was all the food? Dear folks, the food was in homes, gardens, local fields, and forests. It was near kitchens, near tables, near bedsides. It was in the pantry, the cellar, the backyard."

– JOEL SALATIN –

The other reality is that it is difficult to feel known in the often-isolating work of motherhood. In many cases, our neighborhoods aren't full of kids, there may be few other women home, and with families strewn across the country, a grandmother or aunt can no longer be counted on to offer a help-ing hand. Women getting together to can or quilt while their children play together outside is a rarity. Most of us get our advice on the domestic arts from YouTube or Martha Stewart instead of from a neighbor or close relative.

And what about the second question? Do mothers know their job is important? Not always. Radical feminism has long promulgated the idea touted by Germaine Greer that children are simply brought up—they will be no different if they have two parents or no parents, they just grow. Fifty years of collective research shows that Germaine was emphatically wrong, but the attitude has stuck. Without mincing words, Friedan also took a hammer to mothering by explicitly stating that a life spent taking care of one's children is a life wasted. Even today, these lingering messages whisper to women that their job is not only unimportant but a squandering of their time and gifts.

The idea of homemaking is often closely associated with the notion that a woman is making herself a slave to her husband and children. Yet we don't vilify the demands of a hobby or an employer. Consider how something like gardening, which can be a full-time job of weeding, fertilizing, watering, pruning, and so on, is not viewed as demeaning, nor is the demanding boss who asks an employee to spend extra hours at the office. The apparent rewards, such as the joy of growing one's food or of bringing home a paycheck, render the service worthwhile. Yet the work of nurturing, loving, shaping, and caring for those whom we love most is often assumed to be oppressive to the will, freedom, and flourishing of the woman doing the work. This double standard is evidence that something is culturally amiss.

A Measurement of Progress from . . . Somewhere

As for the last criteria? Does a stay-at-home mom feel like she is progressing in some area, and does she have a way to measure that? Looking at trends in homemaking, one very real change has been the relative ease that our culture and economic status affords. We don't have to sew our own clothes, knit our own socks and sweaters, or grow our own food in our kitchen garden. We also don't have to consult friends or family about canning and food preservation because we don't actually have to preserve food for the winter. Even with the renewed interest in domestic arts, there is still a wide chasm between dabbling in making bone broth and actually needing to regularly darn someone's socks.

Without the daily necessity of more skill and craft-based aspects of motherhood, today's iteration of homemaking is largely dotted with very mundane and routine tasks—pulling together a quick meal and cleaning it up, washing and folding laundry, keeping the house clean, and driving children to various activities. But among these regular tasks, few among us would call them a "practice" as defined by philosopher Alasdair MacIntyre.

A practice is a work that requires honing a skill and learning new techniques while growing in virtue as the work is performed. Think, for example,

of the tradition of a master tailor, for whom boys would apprentice for many years, slowly learning the craft. In learning about fabric, precise cutting, and human anatomy, they also learned the virtues of patience, attention, perseverance, and obedience, in addition to experiencing the joy of doing something with their hands and mind and achieving new benchmarks in their abilities.

For the woman who is task oriented and wants to have a sense that her work is important and meaningful, in homemaking today there can be very little to hang onto. No homemaker has ever gotten excited about her progress in driving skills because of the increased hours spent shuttling children. No homemaker takes pride in how deftly she can sort whites from darks and how quickly she can get wet clothing into the dryer. These kinds of mindless activities cannot constitute anything resembling a practice. The rush to help women break out of the home coincided with the automation of the arts once relegated to homemaking. This, coupled with numerous childcare options and the nanny state, has left the contemporary homemaker wondering if her efforts are all that necessary.

Seeking Validation

University of Virginia sociologist W. Bradford Wilcox has discovered that the happiest women are those who are home with their children but who have some kind of part-time work outside the home. This makes sense given that, for the modern homemaker, her achievements at home are unknown, and her work grossly undervalued. These realities leave many restless and seeking vocational satisfaction elsewhere while still maintaining a significant connection to home life. Work provides a network and engagement with adults that the neighborhood used to supply, and it helps check off the boxes of feeling like she is working toward a goal, such as helping her family financially or seeing progress in her own personal development.

The *ennui* of motherhood isn't the only reason women work. Often, financial needs or a particular gift or calling make their family demands sometimes welcome and other times not. But much of the ambivalence women face in motherhood can be remedied with the support of a loving and attentive husband and a handful of supportive friends and neighbors. While the return to the craft of domesticity that has captured the broader culture can also help with the homemaker's sense of fulfillment, ultimately the undervaluing of motherhood is the more persistent issue.

Curiously, while a homemaker may not engage in specific kinds of daily practices, to make a home is, in a way, the ultimate and most human "practice," in that it is a life spent developing not just a specific skill but the very skill of being a human in full. In the face of its challenges, the homemaker who approaches her calling in a purposeful way is working daily to develop generosity in herself and others and asking and discussing life's big questions in small and unexpected moments. She is also regularly prompted to see the world anew with eyes of wonder, is tested in patience with the intensity and effectiveness of a boot camp, learns how to be an advocate for another, and puts aside her girlish diffidence and narcissism for which she no longer has the time.

"The world cannot be discovered by a journey of miles,
no matter how long, but only by a spiritual journey,
a journey of one inch, very arduous and humbling
and joyful, by which we arrive at the ground at
our own feet, and learn to be at home."

— WENDELL BERRY —

Most importantly, she is getting a doctorate in love, which for her had been an empty, abstract word without the dirty, messy, loud, itchy particularities of this life in close quarters. And she is consoled and astounded, time and again, with the beauty, purpose, and enduring consequence of building lives through the universal language of home.

Reconnecting Home with Homemakers

While the emphasis of the first volume of *Theology of Home* was on the elements of the home, here we would like to look more carefully at the homemaker, the one who provides the connective tissue between the material of the home and those who abide in it. We want to examine *motherhood*, both physical and spiritual. We do this through our own observations and experiences, but also by interviewing several heroic women with powerful stories.

There is a wide gap between loving the home and embracing the concept of homemaking. Rather than merely a box for souls to be stored, home is where body and soul are nourished, protected, comforted, and known. We long for a beautiful home because we long for a beautiful life. But this

yearning will not be satisfied on a purely material level, and the attempts to do so fall short of the mark far more than a humble-but-cared-for and spiritually rich home. Such a home requires the careful hands of a gardener, the mind of a multitasker, a heart attuned and attentive to the needs of loved ones, and the exercise of spiritual gifts which come from a deep and abiding relationship with God.

———————

> "Each woman who lives in the light of eternity can fulfill her vocation, no matter if it is in marriage, in a religious order, or in a worldly profession."
>
> – EDITH STEIN –

———————

Homes that are truly lived in won't always be ones of picture-perfect curation, but rather, they can, despite some occasional chaos, express their perfection as places where the very robust and real activity of family life can belong and flourish.

This book is an invitation to reconnect the dots between home and homemaking, to help us hardwire the concepts of homemaking as the deeply purposeful art of sheltering and nurturing the souls of others, offering them a place to grow into the people God intends them to be.

There is much more to us, our homes, and homemaking than simply the need for outside affirmation and career goals. Fundamentally, homemaking offers an opportunity that is difficult to acquire outside of a home, be it meager or sprawling, a homestead, a farm, or a cloister. That something is the capacity to be fruitful.

This isn't a book just for full-time stay-at-home mothers; those of us who work also care about making a house a home. Nor is it just for biological mothers. It is for every woman. Ultimately, homemaking is a kind of mothering. Despite what the culture may tell us, all women—no matter our vocation—have been hardwired for a kind of fruitfulness, with a unique calling afforded to each of us.

PART I

FRUIT

CHAPTER 1

From Fruit to Power

"Be fruitful . . ." (Gn 1:28).

These two simple words are the first command God gives to Adam and Eve. It is a concept that peppers the entirety of the Bible, with abundant blessings coming to those who are fruitful, while warning and woe is attached to those who bear no fruit. Biblical fruit, however, isn't of just one variety. Like the fruits of plants and trees found in creation, it takes on many different shapes and colors. But among this diversity, one constant is that there cannot be fruit without good soil.

Soil is a vital piece of our daily life, and yet few of us give it much thought. It seems like mere dirt, but without it, most crops struggle to grow. Over the last several decades, farmers have tried to find shortcuts to help soil render bigger and better produce. Not all of it has yielded positive results. One farmer said that when he realized his chemically saturated soil no longer could sustain earthworms, he knew he had to start over and return to the basics his father taught him. Without good soil, there cannot be nourishing crops, and without nourishing crops, those who are sustained by them will have compromised health. This isn't radical wisdom but part of ancient traditions dating back to the earliest days of agriculture. Good crops are vital to good health.

There is a rich parallel between farming soil and spiritual soil. It's no accident that one of the most important virtues of the Christian life is humility, a word that stems from the Latin word *humus*, meaning "earth," or literally, "on the ground." Humility is a virtue required of men and women alike and truly the one virtue all the saints hold in common.

What is interesting is that humility can lead to power, not in the sense we might most associate power with but still power nonetheless. Think of the legacies the saints left behind despite being humble messengers of God. We still read about their lives and accomplishments all these years later, and their influence is scattered all over the world. Meanwhile, many who sought and attained power in the secular world are all but forgotten, or if we still discuss them, it is often in a negative light.

"However many years she lived, Mary always felt
that 'she should never forget that first
morning when her garden began to grow.'"

– FRANCES HODGSON BURNETT –

Humility was manifested most clearly in the life of the Virgin Mary, and she is considered powerful because of her great humility. Already in the second century of the Church (AD 180), St. Irenaeus referred to her as soil because of it. From this rich soil grew the life of Christ, but so did a whole new way of living by following the Way, Jesus himself.

While today the desire for humility might not be at the forefront of most people's minds, a deep desire still remains in our hearts to do the good. This is the impulse behind radical feminism and social justice warriors. But as we have learned from Christ in the parable of the sower and the seed, seeds cannot grow just anywhere; good fruit does not grow unless there is rich soil. Desire and good intentions are not enough; a necessary condition is the soil of true humility.

Trading in Fruit

Three young women were recently featured on a progressive online magazine. All were very successful career women, but each expressed a discontentment with her life. One said she wanted to just go bake bread, another said she wanted to plant a garden, and the third said she wanted to leave everything behind to go raise a mess of children. What was going on with these women and how is it that they were pulled so strongly by these desires despite appearing to "have it all"?

Jennifer Bryson

Raised outside San Francisco, Jennifer was constantly encouraged to pour herself into her career. With degrees from Stanford and Yale, her professional pursuits became all-consuming. But as she neared fifty, she faced a professional crisis that led her to examine her life.

"The career-is-*everything* mindset from my secular upbringing was simply an empty, false promise of feminism. I realized I had to stop trying to keep all my identity eggs in a basket labeled 'Career.' My answer to the question, 'Who am I?' needed to be something deeper than my job."

At this time, Jennifer, a convert to Catholicism, was beginning to learn more about the Church's teachings on marriage. Over the years, she had seen how the sexual revolution kept unleashing an endless cycle of hurt and broken relationships around her. She found the Church's teaching on marriage profoundly beautiful, even indispensable.

"I began to see how marriage is a key connective tissue in the Body of Christ, which helped me see how marriage and the fruit of marriage—children—are relevant to me even as a single person, since I too am part of the Body of Christ."

"God began showing me ways I could use the relatively abundant free time on my hands as a single person to support the institution of marriage. Through this, I have been experiencing a new fruitfulness in life, even though I remain alone."

Through prayer, Jennifer saw how she could serve marriage and family at her parish by teaching Sunday school.

"Working with children was not my idea! It was God's. I was not used to being around children and found this task sometimes more challenging than when I taught army colonels and generals at the US Army War College. But it was a beautiful experience, and in guiding these children to their first Communion, the experience was *fruitful*."

Jennifer's commitment to strengthen marriage and family then found another outlet.

"In 2019, I discovered an amazing Austrian Catholic writer, Ida Friederike Görres (1901–1971), whose extensive, rich work on marriage and many aspects of her Catholic faith is barely known in English today."

Jennifer was so struck by Görres, she has been working on translating her work into English.

"In her beautiful 1949 book *On Marriage and on Being Single: Four Letters*, Ida Görres writes in a letter to a single woman, 'Believe me: no one is created for himself. Each is for others: not "in general," even less so for "humanity"—no, for very specific individuals, whom one should serve.'"

Görres herself was married but never had children of her own. In her writings, she emphasized the essential importance of remaining open to new life in marriage. At the same time, she wrote beautifully about married couples who were never blessed with children, a pain she knew all too well. "Marriage is not my life and your life; rather, it is our life, a new one. Every marriage is its own first fruit, even before a child, and as long as it bears this crop, it is not unfruitful, even if children are denied."

Jennifer said she applies this now in her own life even as a single person, looking for ways her relationship with God can be one that bears fruit.

"Mary's yes brought Christ into the world," Jennifer says. "So now I ask Mary to pray for me, that God would help me see ways my life as a single person can be fruitful by bringing a bit of Jesus into the world."

In the 1960s, our culture traded in the notion of fruitfulness while offering us the promise of power and control. To talk about fruitfulness today is challenging. It feels archaic, obscure, unfamiliar. We've grown accustomed to being motivated by seeing results and having clear indicators of the work we have accomplished, even if it is just money in our pockets. Helping to control and order the life around us can be a healthy goal when balanced, but when elevated to an end in itself, everyone will suffer. But the desire for fruitfulness, however culturally foreign and clumsily articulated, remains a desire sewn into the soul of women and will eventually find a way to express itself in one form or another.

Fruitfulness is one of the mysteries of human life—embedded in the earth with soil, seeds, weather, and seasons, but mimicked profoundly in human life. Human biology, psychology, and spirituality all reflect a kind of ecology of fruitfulness. We live through different seasons of life, experiencing everything from barrenness to abundance. But the Christian story tells us over and over

---

"The world is just as harsh
a taskmaster as any other lord, and in
the end it's a lord without mercy."

– SIGRID UNDSET –

---

again that all things can be made fruitful, or purposeful, even in the seemingly most powerless among us. We don't need the trappings of power to be fruitful. In fact, it is usually quite the opposite. Our fruitfulness is more abundant the more we recognize our need.

Category Change

This category change from fruit to power restructured the way women think about their lives, their work, their family, and their time. Control over our own lives, our relationships with men, our careers, and our fertility was promised as the path to liberation. We can see crumbs of it dotting the cultural landscape in how we speak to and encourage other women today in phrases like "girl power," "strong is the new pretty," "be fierce," and "empowerment." Each of these slogans serve to reinforce the idea that the pursuit of power is the preeminent business of womanhood.

Because we are so accustomed to these messages, it is easy to hear them and think they are innocuous. They reveal an inordinate emphasis on power and strength. The overriding message sent to women through mass media,

book titles, movie scripts, and political messaging is that we must be tough and powerful. This is new. That a woman was "tough as a whore" was never meant to be a compliment, as it denoted a woman who had been hardened by the world, broken by it so that she developed a thick skin to hide her vulnerabilities, while simultaneously using her sexuality to control others. Today, we have come to applaud women for their toughness and power while neglecting the sad things that made them tough. We look at the exterior trappings while ignoring the interior wounds.

This alluring new idol of power meant to overcome women's weaknesses spread like wildfire. The underlying premise stated that power was something men had and women didn't; to enact justice, women needed to get it in equal drafts. The shift was subtle, seductive, emboldening, and energizing. But this striving for power, rather than satisfying broken and hungry souls, wounded women all the more. Meanwhile, feminism targeted something unique: the fruitfulness of womanhood, both in virginity and motherhood.

Satan knows, just as he did when he targeted Eve, that if he gets the woman, he gets everyone. And if he can convince women that their power of fruitfulness is actually a *weakness* and a threat to power itself, then he will have succeeded. Curiously, Scripture tells us Eve was tempted with fruit, something good and offered in abundance elsewhere, but a particular good that God had forbidden. But Satan's promise that she might have "more," that she might become like a god herself, was more enticing than remaining subject to the one true God.

Today, just as in Eden, the desire for power has supplanted the notion of the fruitfulness that flows from living in harmony with God. How quickly we forget the very essential role we have in forming children into healthy and mature adults—the very building blocks of a healthy civilization. Like Eve, there was seemingly "more" promised by living outside God's will, and that promise tempted us to shift our gaze from the good fruit we might yield to the good we might acquire.

Gertrude von le Fort made it clear in her writings that women's problem isn't weakness. It is that we are powerful. But in denying our fundamental nature for the sake of an imitation of male domination, we have weakened womanhood and undermined our ability to live in harmony with our bodies and with each other. We are living in a time unlike any other, when we can see the chaotic power of women on display, like the violent destruction of a tempest or the hidden power of a deadly riptide. Women *are* powerful, but power is not our purpose—it is a mechanism, a means. The key to unleashing the power proper to us—the power that builds relationships, families, societies, and cultures instead of undermining them—is to surrender to the will of the all-powerful God, to let him be the strength and force behind us instead of trying to conjure it up in ourselves.

The hidden hinge that can return our actions back to fruitfulness and away from power and control is the simple but much misunderstood concept of service. Fruitfulness is the consequence of our affirmative response to the call to serve. In contrast to the Luciferian refusal to serve is St. Michael the Archangel's battle cry "*Serviam!*" . . . "I will serve!" It is also Mary's *fiat*, her yes and consent to be "the handmaid of the Lord," which she offered freely when approached by St. Gabriel with the news that she would bear a son, *the* Son.

Decorating with Fruit and Flowers

A recent resurgence of farmhouse style in home design and décor has been accompanied by an increasing return to actual farmhouses and more rural lifestyles in general. Instagram feeds are populated by hip families leaving the city for an old home on an orchard somewhere. Trends come and go a bit arbitrarily, but they can also be an indicator of a new seed in the zeitgeist.

The aesthetic of farmhouse style conjures up images of rustic and generously-sized wooden tables, fresh eggs adorning the countertop, loosely-arranged flowers from the yard, and bowls of single-species citrus hinting at the possibility of a nearby bounty.

It is a lovely and decidedly simple aesthetic—close to nature, but considered and cultivated. It's one that feels exceptionally family-friendly, where we can picture barefoot children running in and out of the scene. Like any trend, its implementation can feel contrived or over-wrought, but the impulse toward it, as a decorating style and a way of life, feels like a fitting response to the chaos and noise so prevalent today. In this context, a desire for honesty and simplicity in our homes feels right, and in some ways, necessary.

But regardless of whether or not we install shiplap on every wall, decorating with flowers and fruit is an easy and attainable way to inject simple moments of beauty into our homes. This isn't a novel idea, nor is it unique to farmhouse style, but as a decorating staple, fruit and flowers endure for good reason. The first known practice of floral arrangements dates back to ancient Egypt. The Greeks and Romans created elaborate garlands and wreaths, while conical-shaped arrangements were popular in ancient China. Herb and medicinal gardens were a staple for medieval monasteries, and the Italian Renaissance

saw floral arrangement become an elaborate artform, one that regularly included a combination of flowers and fruit.

While throughout history, formality and styles of floral arrangement have varied greatly, their incorporation into daily life at home persists, though perhaps more often now with the ease of humble clippings and the functional charm of fruit bowls. Their presence suggests a harmony with the outdoor world, with the seasons and locale, as well as a connection with the vibrancy of life.

The clarion call of the Christian is to right an upside down world through the servant leadership introduced to us by God himself, who modeled it by taking on our form, by toiling in the noble and hidden life of family and carpentry, by washing the feet of his apostles, and by embracing humiliation, torture, and death.

Relationships, Relationships, Relationships

At the heart of women's existence are relationships. We see this in our capacity to read emotions written on the faces of others more easily than men, in the areas of interest women tend to study and discuss, and even in the simple but concrete way our arms are made with a slight bend to naturally cradle a child.

Fundamentally, fruitfulness is about relationships—about sheltering, birthing, midwifing, cultivating, nourishing, and being receptive to the needs, gifts, and potential of others. It is like the conductor who knows which part of the orchestra needs his attention, when to tone things down, when to step them up, when to encourage and when to silence, when to focus in and when to let go. Such activity requires really knowing others. This type of womanly knowing can happen outside of the home, in the workplace, in schools, in spiritual motherhood, or in mentorship of others. But while certainly not limited to the home, the home is the natural environment for this sort of intimacy, knowledge, and responsiveness to take place. More and more women are beginning to make these connections and return to valuing home life.

Trending: Radical Homemakers

There is a movement of women in both rural and metropolitan areas who call themselves "radical homemakers." The phrase was coined by an author of a book by the same name who, feeling frustrated by what felt like a pervasive and stressful pursuit of power and wealth, found an antidote in a return to the simplicity of domesticity, and discovered many others doing the same. Her former lifestyle, she realized, prevented her and her family from living more connected to the food they ate and more deliberate about their habits of consumption. More importantly, their former life had kept them from having the time for simply living daily life as a family. She opted out and started a movement to reclaim the title of "homemaker" as something noble and intentional rather than oppressive, as it had become in the mind of the broader culture.

Theirs is not a religious movement, but it is fascinating. It's similar to when women begin practicing natural family planning for health reasons or to avoid the harmful chemicals of the Pill but start to notice how that seemingly minor change has positive effects on their relationships. If something is inherently good, it will have all sorts of good implications and ramifications. Conversely, its rejection is going to have inevitable negative ramifications. That someone might correctly identify one aspect of a certain truth, and reason backwards into a partial view of truth, should not surprise us. And insofar as they encourage and rehabilitate the notion of the fundamental dignity of caring for family and home with deliberation and intention, it seems like a happy development.

Olives

In ancient Athens, at the Acropolis, there is the so-called "Sacred Olive Tree," said to trace all the way back to a tree planted by the goddess Athena, daughter of Zeus. With its gray-green leaves, hearty branches, and meaty, shiny, black, beige, or green fruit, the olive tree is a striking addition to any Mediterranean-climate garden, giving it both an ancient and simultaneously fresh and new feel. It is symbolic of Christ in that it is evergreen, and particular to the general region which is his birthplace. It is a multi-varied productive resource, bearing little waste. Its olives can be pressed into oil for cooking, dipping, and dressing. In biblical times, its oil fueled lamplight as well. It can be made into detergents and soaps and its wood crafted into rosaries, sculptures, and even historically Jewish temples. It is symbolic of God's great providence and of his peace, as when the dove carries an olive branch to Noah to signify the peace God made with man and his providential protection over his creatures.

1950s Housewives

Beyond radical homemakers, many other women are joining throwback movements that seek to promote their version of a proper image of womanhood as one modeled by a 1950s housewife. While this can certainly work to the good, as we can see with radical homemakers, a return to that era seems problematic. While there were many good things happening then, trying to hearken back to that time period conveys some feeling of a shell without a core. It is easy to imagine that the culture in 1950s America, while retaining forms and customs of tradition, was also simultaneously ripe for collapse. The disintegration which came on the heels of that decade was too quick and too complete for it to have been resting upon a solid foundation. This is not to say that there weren't good families in this era, but promoting the imitation of that style and genre to escape the current dire situation for women today seems to be like donning a costume—a veneer without an embodiment. It will appeal to some but turn away too many because of its superficiality.

"When the angel appeared to Mary,
God was announcing this love for the new humanity.
It was the beginning of a new earth, and Mary became
'a flesh-girt Paradise to be gardened by the Adam new.'
As in the first garden Eve brought destruction,
so in the garden of her womb,
Mary would now bring Redemption."

– ARCHBISHOP FULTON SHEEN –

A Historical Catholic Perspective

A closer look at the historical Catholic family looks a lot more like Jean-François Millet's famous mid-nineteenth-century painting *The Angelus*, which depicts a man and his wife pausing in their field work at the sound of church bells to pray. Or like Sts. Zelie and Louis Martin and their at-home lace company that kept the family of St. Thérèse of Lisieux living comfortably. Or like the widowed St. Elizabeth Ann Seton, who was cast off by her Episcopal family and friends because of her conversion to Catholicism but managed to find work as a teacher to support her six young children. In my own family, my father died leaving my mother with four children to care for. Although she had been a stay-at-home mom, she knew how his business worked, allowing her to take it over after his death.

Most of our lives do not work out according to the best laid plans we imagined. What all these examples have in common are how work, survival, and family were cobbled together as best as possible under often challenging circumstances. Even convents of consecrated women engage the outside world by selling products to live sustainably. Truly, these religious balance *ora et labora*—prayer and work—and offer us a similar model that suits the needs of our particular families and circumstances.

What these examples also share is a common understanding which we have inverted today: that work is for the sake of higher things and not to serve an individual's (conscious or subconscious) private goal of self-glorification. In marriage, trusting that each other's work is done to enhance, rather than diminish, the importance of family will encourage all members to grow in generosity and cooperation toward one another's pursuits, knowing that they serve a shared common goal.

CHAPTER 2

What Is Fruitfulness?

I met a friend for lunch shortly after an ultrasound appointment that told me if I was having a boy or girl. As I approached the table, my friend in her pink sweater—making her vote clear—asked the big question.

So?

I happily announced that it was boy. She hugged me, and as I sat down, I noticed a nearby table of ten women had picked up on the news. These women, whom I didn't know and were probably all in their forties and fifties, sat transfixed on our table, taking in the scene in silence and smiles. Seeing that they were so fascinated by my news, I gave them some more information, like what a wonderful surprise it was to be having a child at forty-six and so on. But after their curiosity was satisfied and we all went on with our lunches, it struck me how focused these women were about my baby news. Had the table been full of men, I'm sure none of them would have even raised an eyebrow about my gender-reveal luncheon. Women are instinctively eager to share in what is surely a common, but still exceptional, example of fruitfulness.

While it includes having children, fruitfulness isn't limited to that. It is difficult for us to grasp this concept of fruitfulness because it doesn't always come with a paycheck, it isn't always visible or even clear that it is happening—especially on the spiritual level—and there aren't always pats on the back and public affirmation of fruitful efforts. In fact, mothers of large families can tell you that quite the opposite can happen.

Erich von Neumann, in his extensive work *The Great Mother*, exposes a pattern which is profoundly insightful in trying to understand what fruitfulness is. Drawing from millennia of mythology about women, von Neumann describes a common metaphor for women as vessels—ships, soil, ovens, even the ocean—each of which is referred to in the feminine form in romance languages. The Church expresses this pattern by being called "she." As a structure, the main part of the church is the nave, which comes from the Latin word for ship, like navy. The feminine is defined as a vessel. Women carry others, both physically in their wombs but also emotionally, spiritually, and intellectually in their hearts, minds, prayers, and in the willing of the good for others. Home, a word which is also feminine in romance languages, offers perhaps the keenest reflection of how our bodies and souls help contain others. It is at home where we grow and are nurtured, revitalized and set on our course to move confidently into the world. In so many ways, home ends up being a reflection of its inhabitants—particularly the homemaker—bearing a stamp of the labor, love, and dynamism contained within.

The soul of a woman is meant to hold and transform those whom she loves. As St. Edith Stein wrote, "The woman's soul is fashioned as a shelter in which other souls may unfold." Our Lady exemplifies this model of womanhood. In a litany to her, she is called a spiritual vessel, a vessel of honor, a singular vessel of devotion, the House of Gold, the Ark of the Covenant, the refuge of sinners, and the Seat of Wisdom. All of these titles are clear references to holding and containing.

In Western culture today, we have the mistaken notion that women can be mothers or not; that motherhood isn't an essential part of our being but is merely accidental. This idea that our human nature, that the very thing which makes us distinctive, can be disposed of, and that we can exist outside of spiritual or biological motherhood, is, historically, a preposterous idea. We can't simply step out of it and deny it. Even the infertile or post-menopausal woman still has a body that says "you are made to be a mother"—the way her arms fold, her hips, her breasts, and so on express the concepts of holding and nourishing. This notion disconnecting women from motherhood is a modern fiction.

What von Neumann also makes clear is that because we cannot step out of maternity, women can be defined by the way we act as mothers, even if we aren't biological mothers. There are basically two ways in which we can be bad mothers: we can neglect our children or we can hold them too tightly. Aristotle recognized that vice resides in the extremes, while virtue is found in the middle. We can see that the healthy mother or the good woman is the one right in the middle, who understands the balance of tending to and letting go of her children. Through her years of care, this mother knowingly works herself out of a job. On the extremes, the neglecting mother rejects her motherhood, while the smothering mother makes the child all about herself, thus rejecting the purpose of her motherhood while stunting and contorting the child's personality.

Lucia and Josefina

Lucia and her husband, Gustavo, are architects from Uruguay who have raised ten children and have thirteen grandchildren so far, with three more on the way.

"I have been a mother and professional always. We needed to provide for a big family and we needed both to work."

Because Lucia and her husband had the unique circumstances of being partners in life as well as in architecture, they were able to incorporate the ever-evolving demands and changes of family life with some flexibility as their family grew.

"We were always on the same page working as a team in the endeavor of raising a family. The fact was that we always put the family first—both of us—that was our main concern. If I needed to stay at home for whatever reason, I would do it. I know that that is not easy to do for a working mom. There were periods when I didn't go to the office and instead worked at home, or at times didn't work in the profession at all depending on the circumstances. There were other times that I took newborns to the office because there was a meeting I couldn't miss."

Navigating for the first time these realities is Lucia's daughter, Josefina. She and her husband are newlyweds, and have been balancing the very busy schedules of full-time school for him, plus work and part-time school for her. Amidst all this, they just welcomed their first baby, Javi.

"I'd been anticipating all kinds of change during pregnancy. We live in a one-bedroom apartment and it's been slowly filled with baby stuff. There are now three people sleeping in one room. We prepared practically with baby

proofing but also emotionally, trying to imagine what it would be like. I was somewhat anxious but mostly excited for this life change. And it is truly a blessing and privilege to be a mother. I always pray for my marriage, but more recently, I have specifically prayed about how I can be a good mother by being a better wife."

The emphasis on marriage is a sentiment that was modeled by Lucia and Gustavo. "A strong marriage is the best thing we can give to our kids. Sometimes as women we are overwhelmed with the demands of motherhood and lose sight of this. That will be my most important advice to young women: always put your husband and your marriage first. Be a team. Always decide together what is best for the family and rely on God's grace. Find time for prayer and sacraments."

An emphasis on a happy marriage can be a bit of a contradiction to many messages today, such as "helicopter parenting" or the insidious idea that children threaten the happiness of couples. For Josefina, such casual and well-intended comments at first felt confusing. "When people would see that we were expecting our first baby at such a young age and still newly-weds, we would get the usual, 'Enjoy your time together now while you still can.' It was devastating for me because I began to second-guess everything: Did I get married too young? Did we decide to have a family too soon? Am I already ruining my marriage before it begins?"

However, Josefina quickly realized that such comments, while well-intended, were founded on a misguided understanding that the sacrificial demands of love are a threat rather than a magnification of that love.

"Javi is a reminder of my love for my husband. Having good family support helped us drown the negative noise on the subject. We've also been happily surprised to have the encouragement of my engineering classmates and my husband's medical school classmates, who aren't even thinking about having children. I think it might be because it is such a naturally beautiful and joyful thing that they can appreciate it even if they'd never do it themselves."

"Motherhood is a blessing!" Lucia echoes. "We just develop those qualities that are so specific to us women. We understand what it means to be self-giving and that the word sacrifice is not a burden but a great joy when done with love."

A woman called to spiritual motherhood might fall into the same extremes by either rejecting or not actively engaging in opportunities to mentor and care for others, or by absorbing others into an extension of her ego, thereby using or manipulating them to feed her and serve her needs. Neither extreme invokes the real knowing and work of carrying others that is part of the perfection of the woman. When done well, spiritual motherhood can become an essential and vital presence in forming the lives of others.

"A ship is safe in harbor but that's not what ships are for."

– JOHN A. SHEDD –

Our fruitfulness isn't just contained in our physical bodies but mimics what happens to women on a spiritual level. The physical act of having a biological child is similar to the spiritual fruitfulness we witness in the lives of the saints and holy women, particularly cloistered religious. In these cases, a tiny seed is planted. Initially, the woman is the only one aware of the new life within her. Time, great care, love, and sacrifice eventually bring a child to life, a child who will eventually have a life of his own. We understand this clearly with biological children, but it is more hidden in the spiritual life. It can be witnessed in the lives of women such as St. Margaret Mary Alacoque, St. Faustina, or St. Teresa of Calcutta, who had a seed planted that blossomed into her service of the poorest of the poor in India; today, the fruit of this seed lives on without her, seen in the thousands she has inspired to follow in her footsteps, both lay and religious alike.

Soil, Seed, Surrender

A friend of mine once told me the story of how he was sitting in a board meeting and an associate from India had just arrived. During a break, the man spoke with great pride and enthusiasm, "I have impregnated my wife." Of course, his announcement was met with congratulations, but also with much stifled laughter. Biologically and scientifically, the new father spoke precisely, but offering such a graphic account was a bit socially awkward.

"Blessed are you among women,
and blessed is the fruit
of your womb!"

– LUKE 1:42 –

At its core, fruitfulness requires receptivity. It cannot be done alone. Without actively receiving the seed, there will be no fruit. Fruitfulness requires a kind of surrender and trust between the soil and the seed-sower, be it a husband, physically, or the Trinity, spiritually. Women are the soil into which the seed of life, but also spiritual seeds, are planted. Far from a merely passive role, to be truly fruitful requires an active will to accept the gifts God has given us—to develop, nurture, and cultivate them with a sense of mission and purpose.

Without fruitfulness, we cannot understand our bodies, our souls, our mission, or our relationships. Without understanding a woman's relationship to fertility, all of these become murky, disjointed, and compartmentalized. This is why the abuse of this relationship is such a violation of our humanity. We intuitively know it to be a sacred gift that we must offer.

The desire to nurture others is deep in the heart of every woman—even those who don't know what it is or how it works in their lives, as we saw

with the successful professional women already discussed. Women were made to nurture something. We can see this in the current popularity of pets. Pets are good and wonderful, but the current emphasis on "fur babies" stands in sad contrast to the declining interest in human babies. The desire to bear good fruit in this world can never evaporate; it merely finds new avenues for expression.

The Virgin Mary has frequently been called the most powerful woman in the world, but without understanding fruitfulness, we fail to understand her. Fruitfulness is the lens through which we need to look at Our Lady. If we try to see her through the prism of power, she can look rather inconsequential and saccharine—and certainly much of the world views her that way. But if we see her as fruitful, then everything makes sense. We come to recognize why she is indeed the most powerful woman that ever lived.

Scripture passages, such as her *fiat*—her yes to the angel's request—St. Elizabeth's pronouncement to Mary, "Blessed is the *fruit* of your womb" (Lk 1:42), and "My soul magnifies the Lord," "They have no wine," and "Do whatever he tells you" all are illuminated through the notion of fruitfulness. Our Lady only wants to do God's will, honoring him, with the purest of hearts, to do what will glorify him and not herself. Meanwhile, her deepest longing is to bring all her children, each of us, to her Son.

Also in Mary's life, even though her recorded actions in Scripture are limited, we see practical examples of fruitfulness: assisting a pregnant relative, saving friends from embarrassment by making sure their wedding has all the necessities, spiritually guiding others to be obedient to God's will, spiritually adopting those in need of love and care, and of course, staying close to Christ no matter what the cost. These are all the ways that fruitfulness can manifest itself in our own lives. Mary was perfect, and we certainly aren't, but in her humanity, she offers us a model to follow.

"The great mystery of . . . God is [that he is] nearer to us than we are ourselves, is manifest in the fact that we cannot even be wholly ourselves—in the sense of individuality as a unique divine thought—until we are reborn in Christ."

— DIETRICH VON HILDEBRAND —

Seeing Beyond the Active Life

Part of the reason fruitfulness is a challenging notion for understanding womanhood today is because we are largely a culture which emphasizes the active and visible life, while much of the process of fruitfulness is hidden. The fruit only appears at the end of a long incubation, but its very existence is dependent upon what happens with the seed and soil prior to fruition.

The Peace of Snow

I grew up in Oregon, close to the Cascade mountain range. My family has a small cabin in the mountains, and at some point in college, I started going there by myself for weekends. Sometimes I was lonely, but I never quite felt alone. I was at a stage where I was searching for God and there were few places I felt him more closely than in the silence that can only be found in a snowy forest. I spent hours just walking, listening with attentive ears to the deafening quiet of the snow around me.

I couldn't get enough of it, once even venturing out for a five-mile walk through a foot of it when recovering from pneumonia. I saw coyotes in the distance; I could smell the crisp fresh scent of the outdoors, occasionally mingling with the smoke from a nearby chimney, and I heard the crunch of my steps through the snow. This was my classroom for contemplation where I learned to hear "the still, small voice."

There is something enigmatic about snow. Often it arrives silently, without ceremony. One scarcely knows it is there. Only over time does it reveal itself. The accumulation brings with it a blanket of beauty. Everything becomes different, suddenly pure, calm, quiet, and glistening with wonder.

It shouldn't be surprising that Our Lady of the Snow is one of the oldest devotions to the Virgin Mary. Around AD 350, during the pontificate of Pope Liberius, the Virgin Mary miraculously showed where the Basilica of St. Mary Major should be built by creating a snowstorm in the middle of August. The church was built exactly where the snow fell, measured by those who drew the boundaries before the snow had a chance to melt.

Miraculous snowstorms notwithstanding, Mary, in her maternal goodness, like all good mothers, performs small, almost indiscernible acts of love without anyone noticing, at least until there is some accumulation. Even the Rosary mimics this snowy pattern. One bead at a time—how many lives have been transformed in dramatic ways through those humble collective whispers?

When I read *The Secret Garden* to my daughters, I was struck by how much of Frances Hodgson Burnett's classic tale is a story about mothers. The plot centers on a sad and sour orphaned girl who finds herself in a big manor with little to amuse herself, that is, until she discovers a secret garden and her poor sickly cousin, Collin. The story begins with one bad mother, who shirked her duties in favor of parties, even to the point of exposing her entire household to cholera. Another mother, who died much too young, left behind a bereaved husband who could scarcely look at his son with his mother's eyes. And finally, a quiet, simple common woman, Mrs. Susan Sowerby, mother of twelve, who helped bring the two orphans back to life again.

Quietly and without fanfare, Susan's small gestures, many of them performed remotely, change the lives of the spoiled, sour, sickly, orphaned cousins. Her part is so subtle, she doesn't even appear in the 1993 Francis Ford Coppola film version, but anyone who knows the book has trouble imagining the story's end without the small interventions of prudent, wise, and loving Susan Sowerby. Like small snowflakes, her many acts of kindness culminate in two very different children from the story's start. Yes, the secret garden helped, but she and her children are the real gardeners of the story.

The actions of women, especially around the home, can feel inconsequential and unimportant, but looked at collectively, all of these small, humble acts build memories, and a true sense of safety and of being loved by those who receive them.

We have neutered the power of the soul's interior life. Historically and culturally this was not always the case. Cloistered nuns offer us a different way to look at spiritual soil. For roughly 1,500 years, women who took religious vows were largely cloistered, a vocation which had its roots with the consecrated virgins of Judaic and then early Christian times. To discount the power of the cloistered nun is to discount the power of prayer. Active orders of female religious did not become prevalent until the sixteenth and seventeenth centuries, with orders like St. Vincent de Paul's Daughters of Charity or St. Jane de Chantal's establishment of the Visitation Order, which led to women religious with an active vocation in the world. Prior to that time, the cloistered vocation of prayer provided a great source of lifeblood to the Church. "Those in the Church who perform the function of prayer and continual penance," Pope Pius XI explained, "contribute to the growth of the Church and the salvation of the human race to a greater degree than those who cultivate the Lord's field by their activity; for, if they did not draw down from heaven an abundance of divine grace to irrigate the field, the evangelical workers would certainly receive less fruit from their labors."

This life of apparent "inactivity" is a rare find in our busy culture. When my husband, a convert, first encountered nuns in full habit, he was struck by how vital their existence seemed to the life of the Church. In habit, manner, and mission, they stand in clear contradiction to the world, and it is precisely this contradiction that helps the world meet its supernatural end. Though hidden, they are an integral part of the very engine of the Church.

I have come to call a special group of nuns who I'm particularly close to the "mothers who mother mothers." There have been so many occasions when I've brought my struggles and prayer requests to them. Knowing they have God's ear offers deep consolation.

Such women truly make a home in their hearts for Christ so that he may come to dwell more closely with all of us. They are living channels of grace, engaging in every type of prayer for their own benefit but also for the benefit of the world. They intercede for us, offering themselves and their prayers and sacrifices to God, to bring about the fruit of grace in the world. Their fruit can be both spiritual and material, even though it may appear to outsiders

that they don't contribute anything to society. Like the dark, rich soil in winter, much is going on below the surface.

There are many parallels here with stay-at-home moms, who absorb a message that they are wasting their gifts by staying home, or with the elderly, who can be treated as a burden or made to feel their life is no longer worth living because they are old, infirm, and frail. It is, however, in these stages of life, with numerous opportunities to embrace daily crosses, that there is potential for tremendous fruit, even if invisible to the naked eye.

We tend to overemphasize the active life, largely as a result of our interior bankruptcy. But while those of us who are in the world might not have the ability to spend hours in prayer like a cloistered nun, a rich prayer life is still vital for us as well. We cannot wait for a new stage in life to come about

to spark a life of prayer; in the midst of our specific responsibilities in the here and now, we can find Christ. Prayer can happen over the dishes, while nursing a baby, when lying with a child at bedtime, or while commuting to work. Anytime there is downtime or silence, there is an opening to respond in prayer when the usual avenues are no longer available.

"A human being is a vessel
that God has built for himself
and filled with his inspiration
so that his works are perfected in it."

— HILDEGARD OF BINGEN —

Obedience

It is said that one of the most difficult struggles in religious life for women is obedience. Obedience requires trust in one's superiors but also a deeper trust in God's will for us. It is the direct placing of our will underneath the will of another. Confidence in the superior is important, but so is the understanding that it is ultimately God's will working through the superior. There are countless stories of a woman's obedience yielding tremendous fruit, such as when St. Bernadette was asked to dig in the dirt by the Blessed Virgin Mary at Lourdes. Despite the unusual nature of this command, she obeyed, and her scratching led to the spring that still today provides healing waters to the millions who flock there each year.

Here again, we see this parallel between the struggles of female religious and married life. The notion that a woman should "submit" to the will of a man is so out of vogue that it seems utterly preposterous that anyone should take it seriously. And yet, the example of Christ is telling; though clearly superior in nature, he willingly submitted to Mary and Joseph and eventually to earthly

Apples

Though referenced generically as "a fruit" in Genesis, the downfall of Adam and Eve is most commonly associated with an apple. The Latin word for apple is *malum*, which also means evil. In Greek mythology, an apple was part of the beauty contest among the goddesses who sparked the Trojan War, and even in *Snow White*, a story commonly thought to be rife with biblical references, the heroine was poisoned with an apple. Federal period portraits often depicted mothers carrying bowls of red apples as a symbol of fertility and the family. In Christian artwork, an apple in the hand of Adam or Eve symbolizes sin, but when depicted in the hand of Christ or Mary, it points to redemption from sin and the fruit of salvation.

authorities, despite it leading to his death on a cross. Like the obedience of a nun to her superior or a little French girl to the Virgin Mother, great fruit is produced when we entrust ourselves to our husband's will on issues that fall under his authority, particularly regarding the provision for and protection of the family. There is a common caricature (sometimes earned) of a fundamentalist father wielding power over his obedient, submissive wife, but this is an appeal to an unhealthy dynamic in order to defeat the possibility of a healthy one.

The leadership of Christ is a servant leadership. In a deeply loving marriage, the relationship between husband and wife is one of such habitual and instinctive loving submission to one another, one of such mutual friendship—with all the respect, discussion, and care friendship involves—that the idea of that fundamentalist caricature is as foreign to them as would be the opposite extreme of grave neglect.

Loving the Father

Fruitfulness in making a home emanates from being in a filial relationship with God. Scripture offers us a look at the fruits we can expect as we grow closer to God: charity, joy, peace, patience, kindness, goodness, forbearance, gentleness, faith, modesty, self-control, and chastity.

Cut off from him, we rely on our own well to refresh our souls rather than the un-depletable wellspring available to us as sons and daughters of our eternal Father. We cannot understand who we really are without reference to him who is both the cause and the purpose of our lives, physically and spiritually. We are called to communion with him, and this is a process of continually conforming our will to his. Knowing his will in specific instances requires prayer and discernment, but we can confidently know that, in general, his will is centered on love. For our hearts to draw closer to his, we must have the heart of a servant, for this is the nature of his heart.

At sea, an experienced captain and crew know well that the ship is always a bit off course. Wind, waves, storms, and various other conditions conspire to influence the path of the ship from a little to a lot. The work of sailing a boat or mastering a ship involves constant course correction. This requires attention to both the little details of the moment and the ultimate destination.

It is a beautiful metaphor for the spiritual life. We will always love him imperfectly in light of his perfect love for us. Our affections and attentions are continually drawn and pulled by the dazzling things of this world, things that can very well be good but which can supersede his place in our hearts if we aren't regularly correcting our course. The Church is generous in setting us on a path that, if we avail ourselves, can guide us through our course correction by prompting habits of daily examination and frequent confession, and through the routine yet renewing liturgical rhythm of fast and feast.

This can and should overflow into our human relationships—with our husbands, children, extended family, friends, colleagues. Not only do we need to be course correcting from our attachments to things but also from our opinions, our way of doing things, our ego, our desire to have control. In allowing God to shape and mold our hearts to his, our hearts become neither hardened nor weak. Purity of heart allows us to respond and adapt to the needs and demands around us, adjusting our sails and letting the Holy Spirit influence, guide, and embolden us to draw ever closer to him.

PART II

TOOLS

CHAPTER 3

Contemplation

Women seem to be uniquely gifted with the capacity to worry. We worry about the present moment, about the near future, about the future we may never see, and we even manage to worry about things that already happened in the form of regret. When it comes to worrying, we are professionals.

Worrying appeals to us because it gives us a sense that we are in control of what might happen—that by thinking through what could happen, we could somehow stave off potential harm or damage. There can be advantages to thinking problems through and trying to prepare ourselves for whatever may come, but we can often take it to an extreme, leading to decision-making based on fear and anxiety rather than balance and trust.

Worry inevitably leads to overthinking. In her book *Women Who Think Too Much*, Susan Nolen-Hoeksema explains that overthinking is when "you go over and over your negative thoughts and feelings, examining them, questioning them, kneading them like dough." Too much overthinking, she explains, saps our creativity and drains our energy. What women experience today is what she calls an "epidemic of overthinking" that creeps in when we otherwise aren't mentally engaged. This leads to obsession about even the smallest of things, such as what a sarcastic remark from our spouse or boss might mean, or dwelling on our body image because of an off-handed comment from an indelicate relative about our weight. Nolen-Hoeksema writes, "Women can ruminate about anything and everything—our appearance, our families, our career, our health. We often feel that this is just part of being a woman—that it's a reflection of our caring, nurturing qualities." She continues, "That may be partly true, but overthinking is also toxic for women. It interferes with our ability and motivation to solve problems. It drives friends and family members away. And it can wreck our emotional health."

Curiously, Nolen-Hoeksema did not find overthinking to be an issue for women over a certain age. She introduces a woman named Phyllis as an example, who was of an older generation at the time the book was written. Although Phyllis and others in her generation saw more hot wars (World War II, Korea, Vietnam) and sent sons off to fight in them, many of whom did not return, as well as economic hardships and disease, her response and many women like her was not to overthink. When trouble came calling, Phyllis and women of her generation were able to slough off the struggle by "offering it up" rather than fixating on it. It seems we have taken worrying to a new level of fixation compared to previous generations who endured far more stress.

That is not to say women haven't always worried. We have. But now, as Nolen-Hoeksema explains, we worry more because of the moral confusion in which we are immersed and because of our expectation that we should be able to find a quick fix for all that ails us. The idea of enduring hardship as best we can has become a foreign concept.

———————

"Be still and know that I am God."

– PSALM 46:10 –

———————

Worry as a Vice

Worry can feel like a type of protective armor, offering us a defense against whatever life may throw at us. Women have a deep desire to take care of both ourselves and those for whom we are responsible, and given that we haven't been supplied with raw brute strength to go out and claim what we want through force, we have to find other ways to ensure basic survival for ourselves

and our loved ones. The problem is that worrying isn't actually a virtue. Worry may thicken our skin and act like psychological fists with which we can defend ourselves and our families, but its roots are linked with the concepts of fear and anxiety. Unchecked worry can fuel comparisons to others and open us up to jealousy and envy. Neglect or disinterest in ourselves or in our loved ones lies at the opposite end of the spectrum, which is also not a virtue.

But can worry point us to virtue? The answer is yes, if channeled correctly. We do this through *contemplation*, a related activity, but with entirely different results. It looks similar insofar as an idea is marinated and ruminated over, but the end goal is not a defensive one that asks, "How can I avoid being hurt or wounded by this?" Rather, it is the effort to see where God is present in the situation, to see what he is doing, to see how he is providing for our needs and the needs of others. It elicits a kind of wonder, even in those situations of great obscurity, to marvel at what the Lord is doing at this time and with these circumstances, even if we can't always make out the rhyme or reason.

Blythe Fike

Something that usually strikes people upon meeting Blythe Fike is her cheerfulness, often communicated through her easy and robust laughter. The next thing they might notice is the heap of little children all around her. The two are not unrelated, and both begin with an early understanding that she could trust her life to the will of God.

"I didn't set out to have a lot of kids, but I did set out determined to understand who I was created to be with a natural and uncompromising trust that God wanted me to be happy, and that if I could just find out who I ought to be, that happiness would naturally follow."

This was a determination that eventually led her to marriage at twenty-two, conversion to the Catholic Church at twenty-three, and ten pregnancies, two of which ended in miscarriage.

To the litany of questions commonly directed at a mother of many—"How do you do it?" "*Why* do you do it?"—she perceives the underlying, unspoken question: "Are you happy?"

"I think the question exists because people simply think I'm not. How could I be? What, with all the work . . . the tireless monotony of home life, of mouths and meals and bodies and needs."

For Blythe, this may not have been an unreasonable thing to wonder. "It often felt like a chore, or a bizarre curse, to be pregnant again. I ended up having all eight of my children in just over eleven years. And that's not because I am saintly or utterly docile to the will of God in all things. I wanted to be not pregnant more often that I wanted to be pregnant. I didn't want to feel sick again, I wanted to 'get my body back.' But God, in his goodness and in his love, overrode my plans over and over again."

It was through these everyday challenges, not in spite of them, that she found happiness. And she found it in abundance. "It's a lesson that will surely save my soul when all is said and done, and it's this—that I know nothing of what it takes to get myself to heaven. I am powerless and helpless and a fool. And, probably, so much so, that God just needed to shove this life in my lap because it's what it took to pull me outside of myself just enough to see his mercy, and his goodness. It has been made clear to me exactly how little control I have. And exactly how happy it has made my soul."

We read over and over again in Scripture how Our Lady "pondered all of these things in her heart." Pondering is a synonym for contemplation. We do not read, "Our Lady stayed up all night and worried." We can learn from her perfect witness that worry is not meant to be a default position but rather can be transformed into something fruitful and productive by opening ourselves up to the wonder that is at hand.

The psalms tell us that the one who ponders the Lord night and day will bear great fruit in due season. The first Psalm reads, "On his law he meditates day and night. He is like a tree planted by streams of water, that yields fruit in its season. . . . In all that he does, he prospers" (Ps 1:2–3). Fruit and pondering are not unrelated.

———

"Pray, hope, and don't worry."

– ST. PIO OF PIETRELCINA –

———

Christ offers the woman at the well living water, a water that will not leave one thirsting. Pondering the will of God, the goodness of God, the perfection of God, flushes out the imperfections of our own souls so that we come to know him better. And by knowing him better, we come to love him more. We see our smallness in comparison to his enormity. We feel our weakness compared to his omnipotence. All of these things keep us grounded, focused, humble, and aware of his providence in all things. We can do nothing without him. This living water cleanses our thoughts, minds, spirits, desires, and intentions, making us better soil to allow the will of God to increase in our souls.

Silence

Silence can be a critical piece for contemplation. But finding silence can be an elusive quest in our noisy world. Prior to moving to Washington, DC, I had grown accustomed to plenty of silence in my favorite chapels, churches, and at home. Upon moving, I was shocked at how much effort it took to find a truly quiet place—traffic, construction, and outside noise was everywhere in the city, but I also found it difficult to find a quiet church. At the National Shrine, I always seemed to pay a visit when floors were being polished, a choir was practicing, or the organ was being tuned.

It can be challenging to find silence even in our homes. One of the more palpable changes which can take some adjustment in the life of a new mother is the omnipresence of noise. Mercifully, this change happens some-what gradually as life with just one newborn is also usually punctuated with periods of silent sleep and nursing. But once there's a toddler or two com-bined with a screaming baby, or later the busy comings and goings of teens, silence can become a foreign concept.

"Humility is a condition and consequence of silence."

— ROBERT CARDINAL SARAH —

There is a strong connection between noise and distraction. A sound interjected into our environment pulls our attention to it. It startles us, commanding our attention. These sorts of sounds are an inevitable aspect of mothering. A canister crashing to the ground, a howl from a bump or stubbed toe, combatant siblings, the dreaded whiny voice. Added to this are the stream of buzzes and pings from our devices. Daily life inside and outside the home can become filled with noise—radios, TVs, podcasts, others talking, traffic, and so on.

Being pulled in so many directions leads to a life lived "on the surface," which keeps us from a peaceful union with God and exposes us to worry. Worry can also lead us to seek out noise, since noise can serve as a distraction. Some of the most prone-to-worry people I've known find silence unsettling once their kids have left the nest, even to the point of keeping a television on throughout the day just to have background noise.

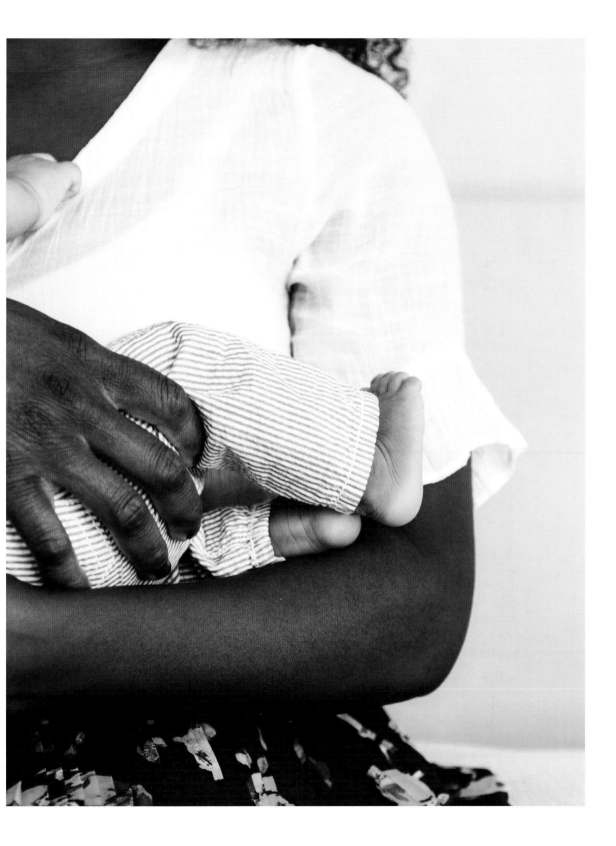

This speaks to exterior circumstances, but interior silence is a reality we are also called to foster. Rather than flitting along on the surfaces of things, being pulled this way and that, a soul with interior silence can be at peace regardless of outside circumstances. We can maintain a presence of God, as though we were diving down beneath the waves of a turbulent ocean to experience the beauty and calm beneath the surface. St. Josemaria Escriva encouraged maintaining this presence of God as an essential key to living with him in the world: "These pious practices will lead you, almost without you realizing it, to contemplative prayer. Your soul will pour forth more acts of love, aspirations, acts of thanksgiving, acts of atonement, spiritual communions. And this will happen while you go about your ordinary duties, when you answer the telephone, get on a bus, open or close a door, pass in front of a church . . . you will find yourself referring everything you do to your Father God."

As life allows, we should seek out exterior silence so as to enter more profoundly into prayer. These efforts to find exterior silence will buoy and sustain us to carry our interior silence into the ordinary noise of the day. On rejecting what he calls the dictatorship of noise, Cardinal Sarah writes in his book *The Power of Silence*, "Sacred silence is the only truly human and Christian reaction to God when he breaks into our lives." In fostering this response of wonder and receptivity to God, we allow his presence to take root in us and we can begin to see with a supernatural outlook.

"If you wish to make anything grow, you
must understand it, and understand it in a very
real sense. 'Green fingers' are a fact, and a mystery
only to the unpracticed. But green fingers are
the extensions of a verdant heart."

— ROBERT CARDINAL SARAH —

Relationships

Anyone in business or politics will tell you that much of what happens hinges on *who you know*. Conversations, being present to another, face-time—all these things go a long way to opening doors of opportunity.

Over the last four decades, advocates for life have worked and argued tirelessly to save the unborn, coming at the issue from every conceivable angle. For many women, however, abortion is something they are open to considering because they do not yet know their child.

The point is illustrated by the story of a mother and her two-year-old daughter at the doctor's office. The mother, having just been told she's pregnant, explains that she can't have a second child. The doctor suggests an easy solution, "Why don't you kill this one?" pointing at the two-year-old. Aghast, the mother responds that she could never do that. "But why?" the doctor asks. "What's the difference?"

Relationships.

One of the most difficult pieces of the pro-life argument is that we are trying to get mothers, fathers, grandmothers, and grandfathers to consider someone they don't yet know. Gratefully, technology, particularly in the form of ultrasounds, has bridged this gap. But ours is not a culture that has long-term vision. A baby changes everything in the short and long term, but considering the future gets trumped by what is immediate and less demanding in the here and now. How can we convey this long-term vision in more tangible terms to those who cannot wrap their heads around the notion that there is a very real and unrepeatable relationship at stake?

Parents of every stripe will still tell you that their children are the best thing that have happened to them. But in the same breath, they will also tell you that they are "done." It's odd given that most of the time we want to collect *more* of what is precious to us, not less. So, what gets in the way? Money, sleep, time.

Certainly, there are valid reasons not to have more children; the Church has made clear several genuine reasons to avoid pregnancy. But do we let smaller things get in the way? Just because something is difficult doesn't mean it isn't worth doing.

Yes, large families are wildly out of fashion. Comedian Jim Gaffigan, a father of five, has a great line about how big families are like waterbed stores: "They used to be everywhere. Now they're just weird." But he adds that his children have made him a much better man (and that he only needs about thirty-four more to make him into a good guy). Parenthood isn't just about the children; it is also about helping parents become the people God intended them to be.

It's a tough sell to get a woman in a difficult situation, perhaps filled with fear, anger, frustration, and many unknowns, to think beyond the immediate circumstances and to wonder about the person she will meet in her child. The beautiful reality of the person who is not yet known is hard to reduce into a simple sound bite. As a culture, however, we must do a better job of loving those we don't yet know because we know we will love them when we do.

CHAPTER 4

Cultivation

Homemaking is not a just-add-water enterprise. In many ways, it is a mystery. Much like growing a garden, we can discover there are certain elements that, if added, will help the process. These elements are often acquired from great effort and through trial and error. Like all virtues, those particular to the homemaker don't always come naturally but must be honed and cultivated so that we might be better at cultivating them in others.

Mother's Intuition

It's easy to overlook the many small dynamics which contribute to the success or demise of relationships. Though all generalizations have exceptions, women are largely gifted with a natural intuition to understand relationships. It is this intuition that allows us to pick up on non-verbal cues, to empathize with another's pain, and to navigate the multi-layered, complex forest of interpersonal dynamics.

This does not mean we automatically excel at relationships; in fact, it is easy to see how some of our gifts become distorted. A sensitive person is capable of being quite empathetic to others, but she can also become self-pitying about her own injuries. Like any disposition, these things must be directed by reason and habit. When done well, such gifts are indispensable to the well-functioning heartbeat of a family and the flourishing of a culture.

Tenderness

In the story *Anne of Green Gables*, the character of Marilla Cuthbert begins as a woman who, while good and dutiful, has allowed life's circumstances to callous her. She isn't harsh so much as stoic and self-protective. In the experience of taking in Anne, she is forced into close quarters with an ardent force of life. Enlivened by this relationship, she softens, culminating in a display of vulnerability and tenderness in the face of life's fragility: "Oh, Anne, I know I've been strict and harsh with you maybe—but you mustn't think I didn't love you as well as Matthew did, for all that. I want to tell you now when I can. It's never been easy for me to say things out of my heart, but at times like this it's easier. I love you as dear as if you were my own flesh and blood and you've been my joy and comfort ever since you came to Green Gables." Disarmed by Anne's innocence and childlike love, Marilla finally lets her guard down and, though not a biological mother, becomes a mother nonetheless.

"A mother's arms are made of tenderness
and children sleep so soundly in them."

— VICTOR HUGO —

Tenderness is a word which can conjure an image of a sappy Precious Moments statue, but it signifies a deep and vital reality. In medicine, tenderness refers to a wounded area that only hurts when pressed upon. It is a wound that requires interaction in order to be known, and one that has not yet been hardened in self-protection.

In an analogous way, we know another's pain or weakness, small or large, by interacting with them. Tenderness is a virtue that allows us to do so gently—to treat delicate things delicately. But we have to first know our own vulnerability in order to respond with care to another's. This was a difficult lesson I learned when I was fifteen.

As my father was entering the last stages of pancreatic cancer, I offered to massage his feet, which were dry and cracked from his medications. Having been used to massaging my mother's feet, I used too much pressure, causing him considerable pain in his tumor-ridden body. While it is a painful memory of one of my last interactions with him, it made me realize that there is a difference between *our desire to help and what is actually helpful.* I see this now with my own children as they try to help with the new baby. I find myself saying, quite often, "Helping is about what the baby needs, not what you would like."

We can grow in tenderness through motherhood, caring for the delicate wobbling head of a newborn, keeping tiny fingers warm, and changing countless diapers, but it doesn't end there. Tenderness is a hunger in every person from birth to adolescence to ageing parents and everyone in between. It is received like a warm balm to the soul. Without it, the soul becomes jaded and calloused. Because our culture doesn't emphasize its value, at first it can be as awkward as young teens learning to dance; yet over time, it becomes second nature, drawing out the better part of us.

Kathleen Wilson

Kathleen Wilson didn't begin her adult life thinking about children. With a career in Manhattan, children were the last thing on her mind when she married David. But early in their marriage, three biological children came along in quick succession. Then, while already in the throes of raising little ones, they took in two foster children, temporarily, they thought. But in short order, these children were put up for adoption, so Kathleen and David adopted them. Overnight, their little family swelled to five children, three and under.

And they didn't stop there. Eventually, they would come to adopt seven more children, making them a family of fourteen. Kathleen, who was always pro-life, credits the generosity of other women in helping her navigate motherhood and faith, eventually leading her to the Catholic Church.

"I witnessed firsthand women helping women."

Kathleen took that idea to heart and joined forces with some other local women fifteen years ago to found Mary's Shelter, an innovative effort to support women in crisis pregnancies. Unlike most temporary crisis pregnancy homes, Mary's Shelter offered shelter for the pregnant woman and any other children for up to three years, including opportunities for childcare, education, and employment. It is such a successful model that other communities around the country are copying it.

Mary's Shelter's first resident was a Chinese woman whose husband was a diplomat in the United States. He returned to China, but because she was pregnant with the couple's second child, she knew she would be forced to have an abortion upon returning. Mary's Shelter was able to help

her until the child was born and she and the baby were then reunited with her husband in China.

The shelter has since seen hundreds of women come and go, many of whom are caught up in difficult situations. Mary's Shelter has strict rules and tries to give its residents basic skills to help them be better moms. "Very few of these women aren't great mothers. It is an inborn instinct," says Kathleen. "But even over the last fifteen years, the culture has changed a lot and the challenges are steeper. If I had to guess, I would say that nearly 80 percent of these women come from extremely dysfunctional backgrounds."

What these women need is mothering, and Kathleen does plenty of it. At first, many of the residents resent the coaching and rules, but over time, especially once they move out on their own again, these women often come to realize how much Kathleen and the other women at Mary's Shelter have done to support them.

When people ask how Kathleen managed all this, especially when she still had plenty of children at home, she says that she couldn't have done it without the support of her kids. They helped babysit and moved residents in and out, they stayed overnight at the hospital when babies were born. "It was the only way I could have done it, with the support of my own family. They weren't an obstacle, but the means through which we have been able to support so many women and their families."

"At the end of the day," Kathleen says, "when it comes to our children, our residents and their children, we just love them all. Even the ones who are hard to love."

And that makes all the difference.

True Care for the Person

St. Josemaría Escriva tells a story of a sick nun to whom he was ministering to sacramentally. In commenting about the care she was receiving from the other sisters, she said with sad resignation, "Yes, they treat me with 'charity' here, but my mother used to look after me with affection." This story served to make the larger point that for a Christian, there should be no distinction within the realm of charity—that real charity springs from a heart of love for Christ and that the merely dutiful performance of charity is woefully insufficient. But the story also points to the reality that being cared for with a motherly love, with true and deep affection and tenderness, is the difference between a clinical environment and the environment of a home. It is often said that the Church should be like a field hospital; even more should it be like a home.

"Gardeners are good at nurturing, and they have a great quality of patience, they're tender. They have to be persistent."

— RALPH FIENNES —

This idea of the fullness of charity, which includes affection, wove a common thread in the history of the Church. As our mother, and with Christ as our head, the Church's mission to care for the needs of the poor, the widowed, and the orphaned was a call to care as a mother for her children. Animated by this revolutionary call to love, the Church, even prior to Constantine's conversion to Christianity in the fourth century, had already begun an internally organized system of charity to those in need, regardless of religious affiliation. Having entered into a pagan empire with rampant infanticide, concubinage, slavery, and gladiatorial games, Holy Mother Church began transforming culture through the distinctly Christian emphasis on fidelity and permanence

in marriage, the solidarity of mankind, and the dignity of each person. It was this love that Christians poured out to others, believers or not, that led many to conversion.

Quite notably serving this mission of the Church was St. Vincent de Paul, a priest in the 1600s who had grown up in poverty, was captured and sold as a slave, and later escaped and dedicated his life to service and evangelization. He established hospitals and ministered to convicts. Eventually, his mission grew so large that he established the Ladies of Charity, a lay institute of women to help run the many ministries, and later the Daughters of Charity, a religious order for women. This legacy continues today all over the world and includes not only hospitals and orphanages but also schools, homes for the elderly, aid to the poor, dying, and mentally disabled, homes for single women, and formation for laity and clergy.

Another outgrowth of the radical call to serve was embodied in the person of St. Teresa of Calcutta and the Missionaries of Charity. Into the Indian cultural caste system, which deemed the poorest of the poor the "Untouchables," came these women religious devoted to Christ and to the downtrodden. A journalist who profiled Mother Teresa, upon watching her carefully cleaning the maggot-infested wounds of a man, remarked aloud, "I couldn't do that for a million dollars." She is said to have immediately replied, "I couldn't either."

Theirs was not a mission that could be explained or animated by anything less than the person of Christ. In further confirmation of the primacy of Christ in her life and mission, when one of the sisters complained that she was simply unable to complete all of the day's tasks, Mother Teresa told her to add an extra hour of prayer in adoration to her morning to resolve this. Though we know (or think we know) the efficacy of a dedicated and devout prayer life, still it is tempting to be preoccupied with doing our many tasks to the neglect of our interior life. And time and again, we find our efforts stunted, barren, merely horizontal. In the spiritual physics of service, the more deeply we seek to serve him, the more fruitful will be our service to others.

"Ponder the fact that God has made you a gardener, to root out vice and plant virtue."

– ST. CATHERINE OF SIENA –

Daily Mass and Daily Coffee

Anytime we are in a new city, my husband and I have a routine of finding little neighborhood churches for daily Mass. Being in the context of city life, these churches feel both entirely other and intimately near. Up a few steps and on the other side of a heavy church door, we can leave the brisk and busy street to enter into the hush and the home of our Lord in the tabernacle. Silence blankets us as we blink and squint at the art and architectural beauty and join fellow wayfarers kneeling. A soft bell chimes and the liturgical language we know in our conscious and subconscious brains begins. Daily Mass while travelling is a pocket of home in an unfamiliar place. That the divine is entirely other and intimately near is true for all of us, but in the middle of a city, the experience of that truth is accentuated.

A morning routine gives some structure to the day when traveling, and some initial direction to exploring new areas. After Mass, we seek out the best cappuccino within walking distance. Most cities have what's called a "Third Wave" or "craft coffee" scene. This style of coffee has consciously returned to the artisanal attention to detail that has long defined the craft, along with a more personal approach to the entire supply chain, resulting in a process and product that is both more beautiful and more human. Relationships with growers are cultivated and collaborative, sometimes over generations. The roasting leaves behind the stylish and intrusive dark roast tradition for a lighter, more disclosive and transparent style, hoping to evoke the flavor inherent in the variety of the plant, the place it is grown, and the decisions made in its cultivation and processing. That same care continues on

the bar with very finely calibrated equipment for the precise dosing, grinding, and extraction of these beans. The drinks tend to be smaller and offered on a simpler menu of drinks, reflecting an upgraded version of the espresso tradition of Northern Italy as reflected throughout the world.

Coffee first arrived in Europe in the seventeenth century, although rumors of the unusual black beverage had been spread by travelers who had visited the East prior to its arrival. According to the National Coffee Association, coffee wasn't given a warm welcome, with some calling it the "bitter invention of Satan." The clergy in Venice went so far as to condemn it in 1615. Then finally, Pope Clement VIII weighed in on the issue, and upon sampling the then notorious beverage, he found it so satisfying that he gave it his papal approval, declaring it was "truly a Christian drink."

One version of the story of how coffee came to be a staple in the West harkens back to the Battle of Vienna in 1683, in which the Polish general Jan Sobieski and the Catholic army routed the Turks so quickly that their supply of coffee was abandoned. Sobieski had consecrated the kingdom to Our Lady of Częstochowa, so coffee, though Islamic in origin, is very much a gift for the West from the table of Our Blessed Mother. It was a supply which ignited the vibrant coffee culture in Vienna that still lives on today, but it wasn't until the 1800s in Italy that the cappuccino was invented. The mixing of the espresso with frothed milk yielded a color almost identical to that of a capuchin friar's robe, and the name "cappuccino" stuck.

Today, while a single cup of cappuccino is accessibly priced, the daily habit of it is not necessarily. Though home espresso machines abound, cafe quality espresso requires quite expensive equipment and will often still yield inferior results. The good news is one can make brewed coffee at home that is truly world class, often better than what can be purchased in even great coffee bars. With a little dedication to craft and method, some properly sourced and roasted coffee, a digital scale, burr grinder, manual brew cone, and a gooseneck kettle full of good water, a nearly perfect cup of coffee is an attainable luxury. Because of its ubiquity in many of our lives, the elevation of coffee—beyond the mere utility of keeping our eyes open—can be a small way to inject care and craft into our everyday.

The graces of the Mass are necessary, but so can be coffee, or it certainly feels that way on early mornings and after fitful nights. But it can also be a particularly social drink. We invite others for a cup of coffee, knowing that there is something in the activity of this small shared experience that is conducive to community. On this subject, Andrew Whaley, founder of Calix Consulting, says, "Aquinas tells us that grace builds upon nature. Often natural and cultural activities can train us for divine ones. The intentional beautiful work of making a great cup of coffee can teach us to enter into moments both natural and divine, as learning to be present to a friend in a conversation in a crowded cafe can teach us to be present to Our Lord in a Mass full of distractions."

Habits of daily Mass and daily coffee cover a lot of ground in addressing needs of spirit and body, and in large and small ways they point us further to the reality that we are incomplete, that we are made to be in friendship, first with God and then with one another.

Connectedness

After years of studying how couples interact, psychologist John Gottman determined that small, everyday interactions can closely predict the success or demise of a marriage. Individuals put out subtle requests for connection in relationships, what Gottmann called "bids." A bid can be as seemingly insignificant as one spouse commenting on the clouds or a nearby bird. Minor though it is, in a healthy relationship in which two people are very attuned to one another, the recipient of the bid will instinctively acknowledge and engage with the bidder, even for a moment. Negative responses can range from passively ignoring the other to active hostility. No one, minor interaction can spell doom, but the cumulation of these small details can speak to the overall well-being of the relationship.

"A tree is known by its fruit;
a man by his deeds.
A good deed is never lost;
he who sows courtesy
reaps friendship, and he who
plants kindness gathers love."

– ST. BASIL –

While it would be unreasonable to overreact to one failed bid attempt, it makes sense that love is found more in small moments than in grand gestures. Developing a habit of positive engagement with another's efforts to connect, even in little things, requires an attentiveness, an openness to the other. It also requires empathy and responsiveness. In this respect, it is not altogether different than prayer, which is less about what we do than it is about an interior disposition toward God, who vivifies the activity of prayer in us. Grace is

received to the degree that we are receptive to it. The Church being the bride of Christ signals something with the use of the feminine word "bride." While both men and women are called to be receptive to Our Lord, women, being receptive by nature, are especially oriented to this relational dynamic of love.

A dear friend, Amy, once told me that her fondest memories of her mother took place in the kitchen after she returned home from school, when her mother began to prepare dinner. She remembers her mom asking small questions about her day, to which Amy would give small answers. Inevitably,

between homework at the kitchen table and light chit chat, she would begin to divulge something that frustrated her, whether it be something at school or a strange dynamic with a friend. Her mom would listen, taking seriously her every concern.

At seventeen, Amy lost her mom to illness, and those small moments in the kitchen took on a tapestry of maternal love, care, and security that she would carry into her own motherhood of six daughters. In being there and being receptive, Amy's mom allowed her space to meander and confide, all the while being held, but not gripped.

This is the hidden fruit of maternity. Compared to the larger, more public events and movements which fill the timelines of centuries past, relationships are particular and quiet. But their significance and influence to move culture and direct the course of history for better or for worse is undeniable. Even at the end of our lives, what is clearly most meaningful, what we cling to most, are our relationships—with God, with spouse, with children, with friends.

CHAPTER 5

Resourcefulness

Women can be very adept at seeing a problem and trying to find creative ways to resolve it. I can remember my mother studying for nursing school with a book and a flashlight all night at my bedside because I had a high fever. Once she passed the boards, she committed to working a grueling night shift so she could be home during the day with us. Other years, when my father was working long hours at a law firm, out of concern we'd feel his absence, she would write songs about his deep love for us. We would record ourselves singing them on our clunky tape recorder and play them for him on weekends. Her act in solidifying him in our hearts had the reciprocal effect of gently confirming us in his.

Creativity, experience, hard work, thinking-outside-the-box, and rallying the troops can all come into play when a woman sees she is needed. From pioneer women to countless unnamed women today, we have the potential to use a special kind of womanly resourcefulness to help ourselves and others.

Multitasking

Shortly after my husband and I got married, I noticed a pattern in our conversations; I would change topics and he would look at me and say, "What does that have to do with what we were just talking about?" Of course, it had nothing to do with what we were just talking about; I had changed subjects

but he didn't realize it. So I started to qualify my speech when I was shifting gears. "I'm talking about something new now . . ."

A study in the *Proceedings of the National Academy of Sciences* determined from a large sample of MRIs that there really is a difference in how male and female brains function. For men, fiber pathways tend to travel back and forth within each hemisphere of the brain, whereas for women, these pathways tend to cross hemispheres. This means women tend to see things from a logical and emotional dynamic while men tend to use one part of the brain more exclusively, and be more apt to compartmentalize. It also implies that women are more wired to switch between topics and tasks, while men tend to be more linear. This is precisely why most women shift easily from topic to topic while men might still be trying to figure out the connection.

It makes sense that we are designed this way. Multitasking, though universally derided as less productive than single-tasking, is simply a necessity for mothers of young children. In this stage of life, women especially must wear many hats throughout the day, all while fielding unpredictable and often interruption-prone little humans. Cleaning the home or making a meal uninterrupted, even going grocery shopping alone, can feel like a stolen luxury.

"Life is not a matter of holding good cards,
but of playing a poor hand well."
— ROBERT LOUIS STEVENSON —

In response to what can feel onerous, wide-ranging technological conveniences have eased our domestic burden, but they have also rendered superfluous many systems which were vital to past generations. Airplanes, in making travel easier, have made the necessity of life in proximity to family optional. Even washers and dryers, which none of us have any desire to give up, have made scarce the regular neighborly interactions that clotheslines provided. Ironically, despite the efforts to ease life's burdens, the demands on our time and attention have grown exponentially while our daily connection to hands-on community life has decreased significantly.

Besides the decrease in community life, some of our habits of multitasking are exacerbated as a direct result of communication technology, making us accessible at all times through email, text, social media platforms, and even the occasional phone call. Like most things, this can be a blessing or a curse depending on how we use them.

While such large shifts in innovation have made the sort of resourcefulness of the pioneer women seem largely unnecessary, a woman's ability to be resourceful remains, and can even be enhanced by such innovations. Prior to podcasts, I would play lectures on YouTube as I went about my day. Women can now use the many audiobooks to do academic research or to perhaps

Brooke Collins

Brooke is an elegant woman, full of joy, and with impeccable taste. She always knows how to piece together just the right outfit and how to combine simple ingredients to achieve a whole greater than the sum of its parts. She is an ardently loyal friend and a fiercely devoted mother.

She is also a woman who acts courageously. When it became clear she would need to seek gainful employment, she entered nursing school, during which she gave birth to her fourth child. Due to restrictions on allowable absences from nursing school, she was back doing hospital rounds at only three days postpartum. This exhausting reality was not born out of ambition but from a practical response to the needs of her family.

"I did not desire to be a working mom, but I am one nonetheless. It is one of the vocations God has willed for me. I fought against it for a while and steadily realized that I needed to cooperate with what I was being called for. I love my job and have come to love the fact that I have to be obedient to the work God sets before me each day."

Despite a desire to be home, she treats her work with the dignity it warrants, whether it be at the hospital or at home. Still, on workdays she returns from the emergency room dirty, tired, and sometimes tearful. "I come home to a messy home with children needing me. And missing me. My return is met with a particular hole only mom can fill, with animated stories about their days, with complaints about their siblings, with questions about homework, with requests to find their gym clothes, or to sign a test. I come home to a sink full of dishes and a dog bowl needing to be filled. I come home with a desperate desire to have never left. But I also come home a hero. A quiet one."

We can get caught up in either the nobility of career or the grind of it, but the truth is for many it is both, and for a great many it is not optional. Regardless, we can turn what is necessary into what is fruitful by uniting our wills freely to whatever is placed in front of us. In offering work done well to God, we sanctify it. In sanctifying it, we sanctify ourselves. And in sanctifying ourselves, we become more effective apostles for the sanctification of others.

"read" a great work of literature while cleaning a closet or holding a sleeping baby. The line between isolation at home and engagement in the world has gone from a wall to a window.

Multitasking is certainly not limited to the small-children stage. As children grow and we take on new and varied responsibilities, women can be very creative in how we use our time, opting to have phone meetings while on a brisk walk or praying a Rosary while waiting in the pick-up line.

And sometimes, we have to remember the importance of those moments when we need to set aside our to do list and just "be"—play with our children, hold a baby, speak with a loved one, or converse with God.

"If every tiny flower wanted to be a rose,
spring would lose its loveliness."

– ST. THERESE –

Comparison and Imperfection

The hard-won wisdom shared by many mothers is that comparing ourselves to others is a waste of time. Seeking perfectionism in motherhood is a self-serving and exhausting enterprise. The ability to multitask will vary among women depending on temperament and proclivities. Decisions will play out differently in different women's lives, and even at the many different stages within one woman's life. When I brought my sixth child home from the hospital, an old friend asked in disbelief on social media, "How do you do it?" I looked around at my messy house, my sapped, slow-healing body, and my delicate, newborn daughter, and replied, "Imperfectly."

The reality is no woman is going to excel at every aspect of domestic life. Capitalizing on our natural strengths and maintaining some level of competence at the more challenging aspects of daily life are good ways to deal with this reality. When I got married at twenty-three, I was woefully unprepared

for very basic aspects of running a home. Home fried potatoes and bean burritos were the extent of my abilities in the kitchen. It wasn't always on my radar to clean the bathroom for guests. I can now cook and clean with some competence, having worked to develop skills and habits, but they are still not my greatest strengths.

I tend to be visual, so I pour a lot of time and energy into finding creative and inexpensive ways to bring beauty into our home. Even my non-domestic interest in philosophy has been fruitful to home life through engaging discussions with my husband and kids or friends around a fire. My friend, Jess, is a wonderful cook, baker, and artist, and over the years, she has continued to develop and hone her abilities. When we experienced a tragedy, she gave us a considered and beautifully crafted piece of art to commemorate our loss. When someone in the community has a baby or a miscarriage, she prepares an artful and elegant meal. Her gifts are not mine, but I can look to her for cooking advice and inspiration. What was natural to her, she has worked to develop, not in a cul-de-sac of self-fulfillment, but for the sake of others through her quiet and steady generosity.

God gives us certain abilities and interests and they are truly that: gifts. This means we should approach them with gratitude and mission. Comparing ourselves to others, then, is pointless and begrudges the giver. How exquisite that we all have different gifts. And the reality that he's bestowed them on us should embolden us to develop them and serve him and others through them. Our gifts are not meant to be just for us, but only truly become our own when we can give them to others.

Despite our best efforts, a difficult truth is that even with our attempts to develop our gifts, sometimes life intervenes and we cannot devote time and energy to them. Other times, we cannot even keep up with the baseline pace we might have established to keep our home lives running smoothly. Sickness, retreats, family emergencies, vacations, and outside demands on our time are inevitable even if sometimes unwelcome. During those periods, things fall between the cracks and balls are dropped. The keen sense we develop to see the things that need addressing and to take preventative measures to refine the day's events is not a natural skill to someone stepping into our role for a day or two. We can and should be fine with that.

Heirlooms

Most families have cherished heirlooms—items that have been passed down from generation to generation. My husband's family has several treasured baptismal gowns that have been passed through the family for at least four or five generations. One in particular has a rich story to tell, a story that dates back to the 1870s in Sicily.

Elizabeth, born among the noble Sicilian class, had made the fabled mistake of falling in love with a tailor, Mateo. Although Mateo made the evening coats and dresses for the nobility, he and Elizabeth were not of the same social status. Disapproving of the match, her parents sequestered her at home in hopes of dissolving the attachment.

But some were sympathetic to the distraught couple. Servants smuggled Mateo's finest threads to Elizabeth for her to use as the cutwork within her hope chest. Among the items were an exquisitely made bedsheet and matching pillow shams. These served as unconventional love letters from him to her and kept the flame of love alive during their time apart.

Mateo and Elizabeth would survive their forced separation and years later be united in marriage, after which they moved to Canada. Without her servants, it was said that Elizabeth didn't even know how to do her own hair, but she was forced to figure out her beauty regiment and much more when seven children came into the family.

Eventually, the family made their way to Detroit. But tragedy struck back home in 1908 when an earthquake and tsunami flattened Sicily, leaving eighty thousand people dead, mostly in their sleep as buildings collapsed in the early morning hours. All of Elizabeth's family died. She was contacted and asked if she wanted to come back to Sicily and claim what was left of the family's estate. She declined and continued to live a life without her noble status in the United States.

Passed down through the generations, the sheets that had bonded them during their time apart, it was decided, should be made into a Christening gown. Entrusted to an old French seamstress, the bedsheet featuring the intricate cutwork of the sequestered Elizabeth was crafted into a gown in 1965. It has been in use ever since and has been a remarkable way to both preserve and honor a treasured family heirloom.

If we find ourselves at times less able to multitask well, and discern prudentially to let go of things here and there, we can remember that life is often longer than we think, with different seasons presenting different opportunities. Seeing that last baby, now a child, run off with barely a glance over her shoulder is a vantage point that reveals the poignancy of motherhood, which, though once felt protracted, is actually precious and fleeting.

Nesting

Various pregnancies found me feverishly repainting every room in my house, teaching myself how to hardwire light fixtures, or doggedly organizing every closet in my home. The majority of my third trimesters were spent carrying a drill or waddling through hardware stores. I had not anticipated it, but the drive to nest, to prepare our home for the arrival of our new child, was all-consuming. I don't think I realized at the time what a lunatic I had become.

While we often think of nesting as being a singularly female hormonal occurrence, men also experience a version of nesting as they become fathers. Neuropsychiatrist Dr. Luanne Brizendine points out that while mothers are obviously biologically invested in the process of pregnancy and birth, men undergo real physical shifts as well. If the father is living in the home during his wife's pregnancy, he can expect to experience hormonal changes, such as a 20–30 percent drop in testosterone, which remains low during approximately the first six months of the baby's life. Such a change encourages men to be protective, stable, and parental.

While both parents are encouraged by their very bodies to prepare for the child to come, most women will tell you that the frenzy of nesting manifests primarily in the woman. We know what's coming and that the bodily home we have supplied for our child will soon need to be established outside our bodies. Hormonally, our bodies mirror the radical spiritual transformation that is occurring and imminent.

Heroic Resourcefulness

St. Marianne Cope's life was a testament to the courage and resourcefulness it takes to follow the will of God. After her father grew ill, Marianne, having just finished eighth grade, went to work in the factories to support her family. After her siblings had grown, she discerned and felt free to enter the Sisters of the Third Order of St. Francis as a young woman. Quickly, her leadership and relational skills put her in a position to establish and become a head administrator, and eventually be elected and re-elected provincial.

In 1883, after fifty other religious orders declined, Mother Marianne Cope was asked by the Hawaiian government to come operate hospitals and schools for the leper community. This surely seemed like a death sentence, which explains why so many before her had said no. It was also something she had not previously considered, but St. Marianne Cope accepted without hesitation, saying, "I am hungry for the work, and I wish with all my heart to be one of the chosen ones, whose privilege it will be to sacrifice themselves for the salvation of the souls of the poor Islanders. . . . I am not afraid of any disease, hence, it would be my greatest delight even to minister to the abandoned 'lepers.'"

"As I grew steadily more comfortable in the kitchen,
I found that, much like gardening, most cooking manages to be
agreeably absorbing without being too demanding intellectually.
It leaves plenty of mental space for daydreaming and reflection."

– MICHAEL POLLAN –

In 1888, despite the hesitation to send a woman, Mother Marianne and two other sisters went to further serve the leper community at the isolated leper island of Molokai, knowing the likelihood that they would contract the disease and never leave. She cared for the community there, taking on leadership of the hospital and administrative roles, establishing a home for the abandoned orphans, and bringing the love of Christ to a desolate populace. Hers was not a spirit of desolation, however. She encouraged cleanliness and dignity in the community by engendering habits of hygiene and order proper to their personhood. Though resources were scarce, she was known to have been resourceful. To brighten spirits, she would plant flowers and fruit trees, wrap the ladies in brightly colored scarves and dresses, and devise various crafts, games, and activities with which to engage her spiritual children. Their environment has been described as more dismal than a penitentiary, but while others might have felt imprisoned by such a limited and dreadful environment, Mother Marianne found creative ways to transform it. She served there until her death thirty years later. And perhaps miraculously, not one of the sisters contracted leprosy.

PART III

The Seasons

CHAPTER 6

Potential

There is a sort of insight into the value of another human being that lies somewhere at the core of making a home, of making a place in which people can belong. Such belonging goes to the heart of our endeavors. In affectionately seeing the potential of another as a child of God, we step more closely into our own potential as well.

Seeing the True Potential in Others

The expression, "A face only a mother could love," although usually meant as a cheeky moment of levity, actually points to a deeper reality. It is not that mothers see their children in a way that is out-of-step with reality but rather that they are given a window into the true beauty and irreplaceability of a human being. It is a window into how God sees us. Far from our vision being biased or obscured, it is instead sharpened. Real, ordered love is not blind; it is piercing and insightful.

Those who love deeply can discern in their beloveds a beauty that might escape the notice of others. In the movie *As Good as It Gets*, Jack Nicholson's acerbic character notes to the woman with whom he has fallen in love:

> I might be the only person on the face of the earth that knows you're the greatest woman on earth. I might be the only one who

appreciates how amazing you are in every single thing that you do . . . and in every single thought that you have, and how you say what you mean, and how you almost always mean something that's all about being straight and good. I think most people miss that about you, and I watch them, wondering how they can watch you bring their food, and clear their tables and never get that they just met the greatest woman alive. And the fact that I get it makes me feel good.

"Growing happens most when things are young."

– HANNAH GARRISON –

Certainly, there is an aspect of rose-colored glasses for one's beloved, but there is also a real reflection of the divine. God is not ignorant of our faults and struggles, but he made us irreplaceable and unrepeatable. His unfailing love for each one of us is not unlike a steadfast lover fixedly pursuing his sons and daughters as though each were the only person on earth. It is ineffable, but we are given a foretaste of it in human love.

Twenty years ago, my young, poet boyfriend, Adam, asked me to marry him. I remember thinking how he felt like my home, and how much I believed in him. I said yes.

It's easy to think we understand the demands of love, that we're willing to sacrifice and give ourselves to another person. Our first year, we had the growing pains of people learning how to begin to love selflessly when they've never had to do anything of the sort. We were exuberant, but selfish. All will, no muscle.

Then came the pregnancies. At some point in the young parenting stage, I remember sitting together at the end of a Tuesday, both of us exhausted, drained, disappointed in our parenting failures, and stunned at how physically and emotionally demanding our life felt. Other friends were chasing their dreams in New York City, others were building businesses. Life for us felt static. There were so many things we were not doing.

Muji Kaiser

At just three years old, Muji Kaiser and her mother emigrated from Nigeria to the United States so she could receive life-saving medical treatment for what was thought to be an incurable bone disease. They were separated from her father and three brothers for many years in order to save Muji's life. Looking back as an adult, the depths of her mother's devotion and courage was impressed upon Muji. "She was an incredible example of what a mother should be—selfless and loving."

Shortly after her mother's death in 2016, and while preparing to become a mother herself, Muji started the Okaja Foundation as a way to honor her mother's memory. "I learned that my aunt's orphanage in Nigeria, Divine Providence Home, was struggling to keep its doors open. I made the decision to quit my job, become a stay-at-home mother, and establish the foundation with the knowledge acquired during my career working in nonprofit development."

Since its founding in 2017, the Okaja Foundation has raised the funds needed to keep Divine Providence Home thriving. The Catholic orphanage is currently home to over fifty orphaned and vulnerable children and has cared for over two hundred children. Thanks to the support of their donors, the children have been provided with everything necessary for a happy and healthy life, including education up to the college level.

Speaking of her own motherhood, Muji says, "Motherhood has made me focus less on my own desires and sufferings, and I mean that in the best possible way. Having children forces you to put your desires second, thereby growing in humility and love. Since becoming a mother, I have also grown closer to our Blessed Mother. I turn to her when motherhood becomes difficult, and in small ways, I am able to relate to her own sufferings."

She and her husband now have three children within about the same number of years. Though she understands that the idea of not controlling family size with contraceptives is viewed as archaic and oppressive to women, she has learned to not take offense by such opinions, implied or expressed. "I am blessed to be surrounded by many large faithful Catholic families. The joy within these families is evident."

She continues, "My advice to a young mother just beginning is to be patient with yourself as you learn to become a mother, take time for yourself when you need it, and most of all, turn to our Blessed Mother when you feel overwhelmed; she will strengthen and guide you."

Like her mother before her, Muji has found that through devotion to Our Lady, she is also connected to a lineage of daughters of Mary in a way that expands across time and culture, united in a singular purpose—ancient and new.

We looked at each other and, in a surge of grace, spoke about how this is it—this quiet, desperate Tuesday evening, this hidden, blurry tomorrow—this is how God will make us strong. It's wonderful to talk about noble ideals, but we have to live them in all the little, unglamorous ways, or else those ideals mean nothing. From that conversation, we resolved to begin again, to embrace our life with all the generosity we could muster, to focus on all we've been given and laugh off the little pinpricks of each day. And when we failed (which was, and is, often), we'd begin again, and again. At some point, life would bring things that were more difficult to laugh off, but the bond created by those years spent with levity and a striving for docility to God's will allowed us to meet those difficult moments with more muscle than we might have otherwise had.

Life lived in familial intimacy forces us to confront our selfishness without gloss or deflection. The rhythm of sacramental intimacy with God means speaking failures in the confessional and being set back on our course with new resolve and the grace to improve. Being known, by God and by one another, is humbling and romantic and optimistic. It gives us eyes to see our loved ones with optimism and hope, with belief that they are capable of great things, and that somehow our seeing them that way helps them see that potential in themselves. It is not an unwitting optimism but one that is deeply rooted in reality. True humility about ourselves is always coupled with inexhaustible hope in God. I've always believed in my husband more than he's believed in himself. He's spent over twenty years proving me right.

"Mystery is that which opens temporality and gives it depth. It introduces a vertical dimension and makes of it a time of revelation, of unveiling."

– JOHN LE CROIX –

Becoming Fully Ourselves

While we often worry we will fail to reach our potential by spending years raising children, in fact the way we actually fail to reach our potential is by failing to develop virtue. Mrs. Bennett, the matriarch of the Bennett family in *Pride and Prejudice*, is a humorous yet instructive example of an undeveloped woman. She seems to be a peer rather than a parent to her silliest daughter, Lydia. But in Mrs. Bennett's advanced age, her imprudence and foolishness are ridiculous and lamentable. In never maturing in virtue, she never matures. This allows the trappings of society, as well as her own vanity and temper, to consume her.

Women have a tendency to get stuck comparing ourselves to one another. Today, it has been exacerbated by social media, but even cloistered women aren't immune to its tug. More often than not, this comparison is focused on our inadequacies in the shadow of someone whose abilities, virtue, or beauty we might lack. The battle to avoid this is presumably lifelong, even if there is evidence that it can wane with age and the fulfillment of one's mission.

For those of us who are still young or middle-aged, an ultimately insufficient but prevalent response to this is to build ourselves up, to seek to be affirmed as well. This can help quell the symptoms of the problem, but it is a band aid which grants the assumptions of the thing it is trying to solve. If the problem is that one is envious of the success, beauty, and prestige of another, then the solution isn't to just get those things for oneself but rather to see the futility of the entire exercise. What virtue, gift, or success does anyone have that isn't a gift from God? It is in his gaze, not that of our peers, in which we find our inestimable worth.

We don't become ourselves because we pursue a particular talent, though that might be part of it. We don't become ourselves because we become distinguished in one way or another. We become whom we are meant to be by following the will of the Author of our lives. This is how we will find him, and in so doing, come to be more fully ourselves. To not know him is to fundamentally misunderstand ourselves. And to know him is to want what he wants. The seduction of a life without him looks like freedom but becomes a heavy, insatiable demand. With him, what looks like a demand becomes light and freeing. Our very purpose is communion with love himself. We are relational in our essence, creatures invited into the intimacy of family life with our creator. The closer we draw to him, the more we become who we are.

We have to be known in order to know ourselves. Since we are most known by God, it is in light of this relationship that we come to see ourselves clearly. But this is not a mere descriptive reality, it is dynamic and proscriptive. It sets us on a mission and provides the very method to fulfill it. Grace is freeing; what inhibits us are our sins, and the subsequent fear and anxiety that they produce. The fruit is found in a paradox: that the more we die to ourselves the more fully we become ourselves.

The Body of a Woman

There might be few more ubiquitous subjects for art than the body of a woman. At various points in history, we have felt great reverence for woman being a vessel for new life. That her body is of ardent and perennial desire for man is plain, but we have separated the desire for that body from its intimate connection to motherhood. Despite this psychological separation, the shape and allure of the body still contains the whisper of potential motherhood. The disordered modern obsession with the body ironically reveals a fundamental rejection of it and an attempt to defy it.

It's hard to deny our bodies are integral parts of ourselves when we go through such bodily things as pregnancy, childbirth, postpartum, and nursing. The stamp of motherhood rests firmly in the body of a woman—which is to say, rests firmly in her.

When I first became a mother, I was surprised at how connected I felt to women across time and culture. It is a connection that isn't gained from sharing a hobby or an interest; it's more deeply embedded in ourselves and psyches. That first experience with pregnancy and childbirth is monumental and yet common. But the connection it yields between women crosses beyond the physical experience into the intangible. What is undergone in childbirth fundamentally makes two new people: the child and the mother. That the child is new is clear, but the woman is also made anew, now with a mother's heart and a specific mission in the world.

New research confirms that even at the cellular level, there is something far more than meets the eye in the biology of becoming a mother. With every baby, some cells from mother and child cross into each other's body and remain for the remainder of our lives. This process, called microchimerism, is even hypothesized to aid in bodily healing by helping produce collagen, as well as reduce the possibility of breast cancer.

This physical cooperation and biological reality mirrors the spiritual dimension of motherhood, which we might have intuited already: that our lives are interwoven permanently with our children and we are fundamentally changed by this relationship. This has the power to be of consolation for mothers who have miscarried—that their child is still with them, even physically, in a way. A new dynamic is also revealed for the Blessed Mother. Even after his birth, she continued to carry a human aspect of her divine Son within her very being, and that he remained interwoven with her after the crucifixion.

Babette's Feast

The classic short story and film *Babette's Feast* tells of a French Catholic servant, Babette, who lives with two austere Protestant sisters. When Babette unexpectedly comes into a windfall of money, she decides to prepare an extravagant feast for what was supposed to be a humble affair honoring the sisters' late father's birthday.

The villagers, in agreement with the stoic sisters, are committed to maintaining a puritanical distance from the delights of the succulent meal. Despite themselves, they come to revel in the food, and in the process, soften their hearts to one another. In allowing themselves to receive the rich abundance of Babette's gift, they expand their perception of their Christian lives beyond a singular focus on severity and broaden their understanding of God's mercy. Babette has used her artistry in a way that is sensual and beautiful and leads to a revelation about the rich and various ways in which human beings might give glory to God.

"If you lose the supernatural meaning of your life, your charity will be philanthropy; your purity, decency; your mortification, stupidity; your discipline, a whip; and all your works, fruitless."

— ST. JOSEMARIA ESCRIVA —

In considering our relationship to the material world, certainly we can grasp onto things too tightly, but it is also possible to look at them too suspiciously, viewing them as unimportant. We are called to see potential in people but also in the material world around us. Christ didn't come to just redeem us; he came to redeem creation. A vacuum can be created where we, who are called to be in the world, simply step outside the culture and the goodness of creation, relinquishing it to those who would have it be pagan. We take a step back to show our piety and our willingness to remove ourselves from a sinful world, but in doing so, we inadvertently aid in erasing God from the public square. This thwarts our ability to cultivate the world.

In an era of consumerism, it is easy to go to excesses, but the opposite extreme is also problematic where we end up denying the gifts of the artist, the designer, the writer, the Babette, who longs to create, to incarnate her gifts and share them with others.

There are many Babettes out there—women who love to cook for their loved ones, to spend the hours of careful consideration, preparation, and expense to fashion a meal to honor them. The meal, they know, will only last a fraction of the time it took to prepare it, but somehow, that act creates something new—a new space for relationships to grow, new topics for friends and family to discuss, new and stronger bonds for them to carry through life. In engaging in these small and varied acts of transformation, they realize the potential of the world around them, even as they are realizing their own.

"To help each other die well is to help each other claim the fruitfulness in our weakness."

– HENRI NOUWEN –

True Beauty of a Woman

We know posthumously from her writings that St. Teresa of Calcutta was not one to have great emotional and spiritual consolation, and in fact, she experienced impossibly long periods of aridity in her prayer life. This was not a woman seeking to find herself, or fulfill her dreams, or be affirmed by others. Her strength was predicated on her love for and service to Christ, and in her littleness, he made her mighty.

Years ago, I was at a gathering with Catholic author and convert Tom Howard. He was speaking about how he'd recently been struck by a photograph of Mother Teresa in a magazine. He commented, "There she was in old age looking a bit like a walnut and somehow she was much more beautiful than the latest debauched young starlet with her Maybelline mascara on the magazine next to her."

There's a phenomenon where women say they begin to feel invisible after a certain age. I think there are complicated and multi-layered causes for this sentiment. It may be that we are undervalued, and once we lose our youthful beauty, we're largely dismissed. But I wonder how much we are in control of that as well. How much are we defining *ourselves* superficially, and therefore lamenting inordinately the changes that come with age?

We are surrounded by a great emphasis on vanity, youth, glamor. The more we strip our understanding of beauty from its ultimate source, the more distorted and hollow our concept of beauty becomes. A woman, in carrying this trite concept of self through life, finds that in making herself—her ego—the center of her existence, renders herself a slave. In pursuing a limited, vainglorious beauty, she misses out on beauty entirely. In contrast, in her service to God, St. Teresa of Calcutta reflected him, and in seeing her, we saw the source of all beauty.

Women well past childbearing years frequently have a wholehearted exuberance when they see an infant. I've also heard many anecdotal reports of older women having dreams of babies. Perhaps these dreams symbolize a new start or a desire for grandchildren, but I wonder with the passing of time if there is a clarity, a crystallization of what is important to women. When we are in the dusk of life, with all the wisdom and experience, the failures and successes, when the ambition and vanity of our younger years fades away, we gain the perspective to see and desire what is most essential and natural to us. The tempting pull toward what might gain us admiration and small satisfactions feels suddenly resistible and even silly, and instead of chasing such thrills, we come to long for what is most precious and to what we are most ordered towards. In this purer state, we discover our true potential by coming to know who we truly are: people made to bear fruit in one way or another. In its very one-dimensional, secular form, a life pursuit of power is but vapor compared to the grandeur of love.

Figs

In the '70s and '80s, figs were best known, albeit not generally loved, because of Fig Newton cookies. That all changed as they took on a savvier reputation with innovative recipes like figs stuffed with mascarpone cheese wrapped in prosciutto, or fig jam served with savory cheeses.

Today, with their striking, statement leaves, fig trees enjoy quite a degree of popularity as an indoor houseplant. In ancient Greece, the fig was representative of prosperity. The word sycophant is a pejorative meaning "one who shows his figs." The fig tree is said by some scholars to be the Tree of Knowledge, and it is also commonly understood to be a symbol of Israel. It is perhaps most richly featured in the Gospels when Christ, upon approaching a fig tree in hunger, finds it barren and curses it. Its leaves shrivel immediately, revealing, even further, its fruitlessness. The large fig leaves previously might have camouflaged its barrenness, echoing the images in art of Adam and Eve using fig leaves to camouflage their nakedness in the garden. Because of the many seeds in its fruit, a fig is a symbol of rich fertility. Perhaps because of this richness, a tree yielding no fruit becomes a symbol of great spiritual barrenness in juxtaposition to what it ought to have been.

CHAPTER 7

Obstacles

A friend and poet, Joseph Thompson, wrote upon the death of his baby daughter, Myra, "Let me tell you about a story. This is a story about a time of death that came before a date of birth. There was never any other ending. All the characters are kind and gentle, patient and understanding. Everyone's heart breaks. It's happening now and in the future, and they overlap. Words are the only currency, but they're bankrupt. You make sounds from your face that you've never made before. It's a good story, but you wouldn't recommend it to anyone. And it's yours now. You are still writing it. You will only ever say goodbye."

Years ago, when my water broke at twenty weeks with our twin sons, we were desperate to hold out hope that they might survive and too stunned to know that it was unlikely. They did not. A priest came to the hospital to give us holy water. My husband, upon delivery, named them and baptized them. We held them for hours, and the hours were stupidly inadequate. We dressed them. We recognized their faces. Theirs were faces that were known to us, and they were known deeply.

At their funeral, a mother of a friend hugged me and whispered, "Don't let the devil confuse you."

This simple statement became a life raft for me, something I could cling to in the sea of grieving months to come. It would pierce its way into my thoughts and save me from all sorts of destructive tendencies that accompany grief, the irrational feelings of guilt, and the various what-ifs.

Her advice became mine to give whenever friends were walking through trauma, including Joseph and his wife, Helen. The devil is not a gentleman who allows us space and time to grieve. Rather, it is exactly in our weaker moments, whatever they might entail, that he comes to drag us into despair and desolation.

But it doesn't take a tragedy for the devil to confuse us. Even in our daily lives, even during our best moments, he can wreak havoc. He knows precisely which direction to push us, either toward self-glorification if we are prone to vanity or toward despair if we are prone to scrupulosity. As the father of lies, he sows confusion, leaving us stunted. To move forward in hope, the best thing we can do is begin and end with what we know to be true: we are loved by a God who is love. He is with us. We can run to him. His providence is beyond our comprehension. And when we falter, we can return to him with simplicity, confident that he makes all things new.

"If you love deeply, you're going to get hurt badly. But it's still worth it."

— C. S. LEWIS —

Detachment

When I first became a mother at the age of twenty-four, my sister, a marvelous and accomplished mother already, asked me excitedly, "Don't you love motherhood?"

I answered, "I don't know. I just love *her*."

I also remember a good friend, once very career oriented and hesitant about motherhood, remarking to me after her daughter was born how differently she viewed her career. While still important, it suddenly felt peripheral and more like a means to an end.

Leigha Doerrer

Leigha Doerrer is the mother of six children, with her seventh on the way. In 2017, tragedy struck their family when her two-year-old son, Everett, unexpectedly died from the rupturing of malformed vessels in his brain.

Looking back on how the family handled the grief from losing Everett, Leigha can see how much their faith helped them through it. "Paul and I, from the beginning, knew we weren't in control of the situation and that we had to surrender to God's will. We were never bitter and never angry. We actually skipped over many of the stages of grief because, from the beginning, we knew we had no power over it."

Leigha's father, who recently passed away, had little faith and couldn't make sense of how Paul and Leigha were handling the situation so well. Their parish priest told them that after Everett's funeral, Leigha's father asked him how it is that they seemed okay. The priest's answer was simple: faith.

"They know that their son is with the Lord in heaven. That awareness that their son is better off pushes out fear, sadness, and grief, because it is joy. Joy overrides the other stuff."

It was a concept, Leigha says, that her dad wrestled with up to his own death. He didn't have the capacity to let it go. He simply couldn't come to grips with his grandson's death.

This is not to say that it was not devastating for Paul, Leigha, and the children. Leigha recalls how she knew surrendering to God was the only way their family would make it through this event. "Everett died on a Wednesday morning, and I knew we had to contact family, pick out a casket, make funeral arrangements. But before all that, I went to our church, kneeled down, resting my head on the pew in front of me, and begged God for the grace to handle all of this. For us, the burden of grief was going to be astronomical. We were all still in shock and things were only going to get much worse before they got better. I begged God to help me and recited probably a hundred times the line from Matthew's Gospel, 'Take up my yoke upon you, and learn from me; for I am gentle and lowly in heart, and you will find rest for your souls. For my yoke is easy, and my burden is light'" (Mt 11:29–30).

When the reality of their missing son began to sink in during daily life, there were a lot of tears and moments of intense and unexpected grief, such as when a favorite toy would remind them of Everett. Leigha noticed that her other children remained close to her and wouldn't go play the way they had before. Eventually, their priest recommended that they "de-Everett" the house, pull his car seat out of the car and pack up his toys and clothes.

While Leigha felt she wasn't at all ready for this, she knew she had to help the children feel safe again at home. Yes, there were plenty of tears, but in place of the Thomas the Train set went an antique pinball machine. The space for toddlers transitioned to an area for the older kids to use. Now with toddlers in the house again, it has been bittersweet for the family to bring out Everett's old toys, to use them again and tell the stories associated with them.

Everett, in keeping with the Church tradition that recognizes the sanctity of children who die before the age of reason, has been buried at their parish. His presence there, along with their fun memories and an annual celebration of his entry into heaven, has kept him very much alive in their minds, hearts, and prayers.

We can either idealize or disparage motherhood from afar, but a person—small and needy, delicate and demanding—gives flesh and bone, quite literally, to what was an abstract idea. Love is personal and specific, and through the living of it, we more fully understand it.

Like anything worthwhile, it can be painful. The sleeplessness, the relentlessness. It is a revolution in the life of a woman, and part of the adjustment is in relinquishing comforts that we never realized were so ingrained in us. It is a process of realizing our attachments and thereby our weaknesses. There is a fragility to love—the almost paralyzing reality that it could be lost. It is the sheer poverty and need of an infant which forces us to confront our own poverty, thereby softening us, and allowing us to enter into deeper and darker oceans, gently and bravely.

This process is inevitably painful, as letting go of attachments always is. In Christ, for both men and women, leadership consists in service. "The Son of man came not to be served, but to serve." He leads us by the example of his life, which was one of sacrifice, both in event and in totality.

Human beings need to feel purposeful, that their lives are not about themselves. Service can take place in innumerable ways, but there is something purifying about the type of service which is less observed, less recognized. It is more difficult to find satisfaction and reward for our egos when the clear measure of success or applause aren't there.

"The laws of nature remind us that no matter how long, seeds do grow. Push through long enough to see your seeds grow."

– ANDRENA SAWYER –

There's an old Spanish saying that when the mother prepares food for her children, she always takes the head of the fish. In other words, she saves the worst for herself. This does not mean we go through life with a martyr-syndrome, wearing our sacrifice like a crown for others to admire, but still, it is a life of sacrifice.

A strange but very human side of suffering is that we can react to it in exactly the wrong ways. There is a post-traumatic tendency to become peevish in our tragedy, quick to take offense by a good-willed but clumsily worded message of sympathy, or to look askance at another's inadequate effort to relate. We can hold our traumas tightly, perpetually nursing them, and in so doing elevate ourselves to a special status where only we, who've suffered mightily, might enter. Our trauma can become both a trophy and a weapon. Such an attitude is truly a waste, as it means we effectively get the fish head and lose the grace that might've accompanied a joyful act of loving sacrifice.

We can also hold our children too tightly, making our motherhood about ourselves. This tendency might become exposed more acutely once they're grown and we are overly-invested in their every decision, stifling their natural need to take ownership of their lives. In doing so, we become an obstacle in their development. Detachment even from good things—indeed, the very best things . . . our children—is a lesson we all must learn, no matter the pain it causes.

A Hidden Life

Blessed Franz Jägerstätter, an Austrian farmer, was martyred for refusing to swear an oath of allegiance to the Nazis. In *A Hidden Life*, the film depiction of his adult life written and directed by Terrence Malick, there is what feels like a meandering meditation on the seemingly small moments of love, especially marital love. We see Franz and his wife planting potatoes, elbows deep in soil, with playfulness and smiling side glances. We see them recounting the details of the day they met, her best dress, his motorcycle. We see them playing simple games with their three daughters in a bucolic village in the clouds. It is a portrait of the great delight they take in each other.

Amidst this portrait, we hear the backdrop of bells—church bells summoning them to a life of grace, bells around the neck of the livestock summoning them to a life on earth, and ultimately the clanging of chains around his ankles summoning him to a life of martyrdom. All three are a part his one call. It is in this context that we see how Blessed Franz was able to give up his life as well as the depth and beauty of what it was he gave up.

"I am not afraid of storms for
I am learning how to sail my ship."

– LOUISA MAY ALCOTT –

Against the counsel of many and with his life in the balance, he remains silently firm. He is routinely told that his sacrifice will mean nothing; his protest will have no effect. But it is not until his wife comes to see him and tells him she loves and supports him, no matter what he decides, that he breaks down sobbing. His tears flow in part from a transcendent joy. Her voice dissuading him from martyrdom would have been crushing. He has known Christ through their love, and she is sacrificing her life, their life, as well. He knows this deeply and needed the unity of their will to give him the courage to sacrifice their life for Christ.

It is striking how much their harmonious marriage was ordered firstly to God. He was manly, not in the caricature of a man, full of noise and bravado, but in the truest sense: in his courageous service to God. It was his service that made him a leader. And his wife's service was no less brave or sacrificial. He knew and submitted himself to what God was asking of him and asked if she would as well, knowing that she could freely refuse. The same God who was the cause of their happiness was also the cause of their courage and the object of their ultimate sacrifice. Their life together had Christ behind it and in front of it, and he animated it all along. They were deeply alive because they were alive in him.

Relics and Reliquaries

Relics are a quirky but much-loved Catholic devotion. Wanting to hang onto something important from a loved one is certainly not unique to Catholics but born of a human instinct. The material, even the most mundane of objects, can become treasures from loved ones who have died. We savor and safeguard photographs, a favorite Christmas decoration, and jewelry worn by our loved ones. For decades, I kept a Marian nightlight in my room that was used by my father during his battle with cancer.

There are churches and monasteries that boast large collections of saints' relics, such as St. Anthony's chapel in Pittsburgh, which has over five thousand relics, or the Dominican Priory in Washington, DC, that venerates their sizable collection on the eve of All Saint's Day with a beautiful and lengthy litany of the saints.

For decades, as the Church went through post–Vatican II convulsions, many relics and reliquaries were tossed out, literally into the trash. One man in Pennsylvania made it his mission to rescue the valuable treasures from dumpsters, lovingly warehousing them for decades and eventually selling the reliquaries (minus the relics) to priests and parishes. Leigha Doerrer was able to join her parish priest at this man's store, now run by the second generation of protectors, and picked out a reliquary for a lock of hair taken from her two-year-old son, Everett, after his tragic death. This has understandably become a family treasure.

Reliquaries come in all shapes and sizes. Antique reliquaries can be purchased on Etsy, secondhand stores, and estate sales. New reliquaries are now available, modeled after vintage styles, while more contemporary styles, particularly those hailing from Latin America, are available.

And how does one get a relic in the first place? Often, they are handed down among families or given as gifts. Friends gave us a relic of St. Teresa of Avila after they inherited many from a beloved priest upon his death. I was given relics of St. John

Neumann and St. Francis Xavier Seelos by a seminarian who could not take them with him to his new life. My husband was also able to get one of St. Thomas Aquinas in Rome. It is always a blessing to have these relics on hand, and to venerate them in a special way on the saint's feast day.

Relics made from the body parts of saints may seem spooky or even grotesque, but they offer those of us who are still flesh and bone a tangible connection to those who are in heaven.

Abandonment to the Will of God

Blessed Guadalupe Ortiz was a Spanish chemist who chose celibacy in order to devote her life to service and evangelization while still remaining a professional in the world. Her life bore enormous fruit both professionally and for her many spiritual daughters. Blessed Guadalupe was instrumental in establishing numerous residences for young women and schools and services for the poor, and she served as a mentor for her many spiritual daughters. She did all this without it taking away from her rigorous academic and professional endeavors. In her letters, which were published after her beatification, she reveals her very human struggles with orderliness, vanity, and self-love, but her fidelity and trust in God were consistent and evident.

In dealing with severe heart problems for the latter twenty years of her life, she confided, "Last night I thought I was dying, that my final moments had come. I didn't want to disturb anyone so I just lay there quietly. I told myself: I've gone to confession and made an act of contrition and abandonment. If I die, what more could I do?"

There is no doubt that the wide and rich fruit of her life's work came from her trust and abandonment to the will of God in all things, including her life itself.

"God teaches the soul by pains and obstacles, not by ideas."

— JEAN-PIERRE DE CAUSSADE —

When we think of our own lives, there is a particular poignancy to suffering because oftentimes the thing of which we are deprived of is something of great worth. Most of us are not called to martyrdom, but our plans can be frustrated and thwarted in ways we've not chosen. Infertility, marital strife, illness, and career frustration can leave us wondering about God's plan. If what we long for is good, how do we reconcile ourselves to the deprivation of it? Despite our best efforts, there is much that is beyond our control or our ability to understand. Sometimes we might be able to see the fruit of suffering well, other times we might not see any rhyme or reason for what we've been called to endure. Regardless, we can be assured that if endured with love for Christ, and united to him, the spiritual benefit for our sanctity and for our prayer intentions is immense. Deep suffering must be met with persevering fidelity and trust. But these are not things we can conjure up on our own.

CHAPTER 8

Community

Various metrics confirm that over the last thirty years, there has been a sharp increase in loneliness. Almost one in four Americans (most under the age of fifty) feel isolated, with no one they can confide in, according to a 2018 study from the Kaiser Family Foundation in partnership with the *Economist*. Recently in the UK, the prime minister appointed a "minister for loneliness" in an effort to draw attention to what increasingly is seen as a societal epidemic contributing to depression and other health risks, both mental and physical.

While superficially we're more connected than ever through social-media platforms, such connectivity often serves merely to reinforce our isolation. Social media sets the stage for a pantomime of a relationship that bears closer resemblance to performer and audience member than it does to friend or beloved, which demand vulnerability and being known.

But this loneliness trend predates social media. Robert Putnam's book *Bowling Alone: Examining Our Increasing Trend of Isolation* was based on an essay that was published in 1995, when an already alarming number of people were reporting feelings of loneliness. Modern isolation is distinct from solitude, the latter being more like a conscious and positive retreat from distraction. Isolation is more of an omission, a deprivation of what ought to be.

What is missing and from what have we cut ourselves off? As we march forward, what are we jettisoning along the way? From churches to families, from our historical and literary patrimony in the humanities, to our common *mores*—more and more often, we have been saying no. For many not raised with any connection to the richness of such things, the no is not of protest but of apathy. It is a shrug, a resounding "meh" to the depths of things we have not penetrated, a rejection without an understanding of what it is we reject.

"A garden should make you feel you've entered privileged space–a place not just set apart but reverberant–and it seems to me that, to achieve this, the gardener must put some kind of twist on the existing landscape, turn its prose into something nearer poetry."

– MICHAEL POLLAN –

Women, whom we most empower to lead and drive this progressive march, are often the ones most deeply and negatively affected by it. Our liberation depends on severing ourselves from the things of the past. We approach with suspicion what threatens to tie us down or inhibit our choices. This includes not only our biology but also any need for a man or children.

But human beings need one another. Any woman experiencing pregnancy and postpartum knows this is harrowing stuff to go at alone. A child without a father or a mother intuitively knows the depth of that void. Denying our vulnerability does not erase our vulnerability. It merely isolates us, leaving us alone and unmoored. We become lost, and what the lost person wants is home.

With our roots cut off, we are desperate to patch and tether ourselves into place however we can. Home is an object of fundamental desire, deeper than a poured foundation and higher than vaulted ceilings. We desperately want a place with a sense of permanence, safety, care. We want messy and beautiful and real, with bodies and dishes and wine, tears and snorts of laughter.

Even within family life, we can feel isolated. A woman taking care of many children without much community support might grow skeptical of her ability to find a broader community of friends for both practical reasons and cultural ones.

Our fundamental desire for community is pervasive and persistent. It might manifest itself in an inordinate emphasis on home improvement—on Turkish towels, hand-thrown pottery, and the latest tile backsplash. But the thing is not the thing. If we can see through these efforts to anchor and subsume ourselves into material beauty, we might see that though these things are good and worthwhile, they are also sign posts, hinting to us of our deeper need.

Domestic Souvenirs

"Is there something of mine that you want?"

I gulped when I heard the question as it suddenly addressed the elephant in the room. Nora didn't have much time left. Pancreatic cancer was draining the life out of my dear friend.

"Yes," I replied, "I would like the pitcher you bought in Italy."

I had been with her when she purchased the hand-painted pitcher in classic blue and white just before Christmas in the hilltop town of Orvieto. I had moved to Rome and Nora came along to spend the holidays with me. After shopping, a lovely lunch, and time in a church which boasted a Eucharistic miracle, we made our way back to Rome. As we walked home in the darkness, a thief hanging out of a car rounded a bend at the Colosseum and snatched her handbag. We raced after the vehicle, but it quickly melted into a sea of red taillights. Giving up our chase, I heard her panting, "Praise God, Praise God." It was the third time she had been mugged, she told me later, and she wanted to get her response to it right. Rather than anger and fear, she wanted to praise God in all things. Her charming pitcher reminds me of all this now when it adorns my table.

My table is also full of other memories. I have the pale pink and cream china that had been my grandmother's. It reminds me of her kitchen, often warmed by a waist-high fireplace, where we gathered as a family for so many meals. It was the place where family lore was shared, like when my uncle helped himself to the center of a banana cake and replaced the cover, only for it to be later served, to my grandmother's horror, at her ladies' luncheon. Her dishes remind

me of her tender smile, not untouched by suffering, and her constant love that was like the gentle embers in her fireplace.

There are also the cloth napkins I bought for my mother in southern France as a college student. She didn't tell me then that she didn't like cloth napkins, but years later, to my delight, she passed them back to me in mint condition. Their sunny yellow remind me that she has never been one to complain or speak ill of others and that my childhood was marked by her cheerfulness, even on the grayest of rainy Oregon days.

Our dining room has many family treasures, hand-etched crystal, antique chairs, champagne glasses, teacups, and a blend of milk glass china from both sides of the family. There is a chafing dish from my parent's wedding and silver flatware engraved with tiny rosebuds. All of these items, curated by the women who labored to make my husband and me who we are, carry the echoes of those who treasured them before. They are reminders of fits of laughter, tears of sorrow, and the imperfect jostlings of souls trying their best to love each other through life's feasts and fasts.

These items make me think of these women who love me deeply and whom I deeply love. I think about who they were and what they were thinking as they selected them or received them as a gift. Their crystal, glass, and silver are much less complicated than some of the other items I have inherited from them, like my grandmother's nose and my mother's mouth and chin, making it easier to delight in their present and savor their past.

At a time when people are abandoning family heirlooms, I'm holding tightly to mine. They offer, in small and sweet ways, a tactile reminder of the women who, like Christ, gave generously of themselves so that we might have life, and have it abundantly.

They are whispers and shadows of our longing for a kind of beauty that is a continuum of sacrificial love and generation, permanence and lineage, linking us to past and present and to one another, as well as to a destination somewhere just ahead.

> "What a great favor God
> does to those he places
> in the company of
> good people."
>
> – ST. TERESA OF AVILA –

Community of Friendship

In the often-harrowing transition into motherhood, I was plagued with uncertainty about everything from my new identity to what, or if, to employ a sleep training method. Advice came from every corner, crossing and contradicting each other. I was alone a lot with my baby, often never leaving our apartment due to exhaustion or intimidation about the inevitable crying and diaper disasters. And, having moved to a new town, social opportunities were scarce.

When my second baby came, I happened upon a local daily Mass where I spotted a lovely young woman, a stranger to me, who was carrying a baby boy as well. After Mass, she approached me in the parking lot to introduce herself. Her name was Hope. She had kind eyes and a warm, casual manner. She explained she was from Vermont and new to the area as well. Hastened by the chaos of crying babies, we quickly exchanged numbers, and nothing would've likely come from it but for her. She initiated a call and then an invitation to a park group she'd discovered.

Humor

Good humor and the benefit of fun can be underrated aspects of life. But while it would be inappropriate to laugh at a funeral, it would also be unfitting to walk around with a somber or overly-serious demeanor during normal activities. There is a high correlation between the inability to laugh at oneself and the tendency to be insufferable.

If we allow it, family life can lend itself to much mirth because of the sheer number of ridiculous things that are said and done. In our family, we've not kept baby books, but for years we have diligently recorded every funny thing a family member has said. Unimaginatively titled our "Funny Things Book," it is trotted out on a whim during a family dinner here and there so we can all shriek and reminisce about our moments of levity. The smaller kids have an easy and eager audience in older siblings who find robust delight in their younger siblings' silliness, intentional or otherwise.

Additionally, a family will be far more lighthearted if the parents are light with one another. Granted there are more important things to emphasize for a good marriage, but making a marriage fun is of more consequence than we might think. Devoting time and space to being playful with one another, as life and circumstance afford, is vital. We are wired to desire happiness and are naturally drawn to the refreshment found in a cheerful relationship. This tone, set by husband and wife, engenders a more cheerful family life and sets a model for what children should foster in their future families as well. There are a lot of reasons children leave the faith. As much as is within our power, we should strive not to add to that list by presenting them with a pervasively dour embodiment of Christian life.

This park group became my formation into motherhood. We met weekly, and as most of us were homeschoolers, these weekly meetings lasted over a decade. When other park groups disbanded because the school years began, we continued. Many of us would remark at how we looked forward all week to those long, lingering Friday afternoons where we would trade recipes, share setbacks, encourage each other, and wrestle with life's problems, big and small. It was humbling and beautiful navigating through life with such sincerity and intimacy. Sometimes those afternoons would stretch into evening until whining children and waning daylight would finally prompt a scramble into car seats for baths and dinners at our respective homes. Many of those women and their husbands are still entwined beautifully in our life and serve as spiritual moms and dads to our six children.

"Solemnity flows out of men naturally,
but laughter is a leap.
It is easy to be heavy: hard to be light.
Satan fell by the force of gravity."

– G. K. CHESTERTON –

Hope remains a soul sister to me, and I hate to think of what wouldn't have been had she not approached this stranger in the parking lot. In those early, challenging mothering years, when I felt frustrated or selfish and unsure of how to navigate life's demands, I'd often think of how I'd seen her relate to her children and try to imitate her patience and generosity. Eventually, my imitation became more an embodiment; my instincts toward impatience or exasperation faded as new ways and habits formed. The power of women to influence one another is profound. We are affected for ill or for good by the company we keep. Bitterness is contagious, as is kindness. As is Hope.

My motherhood began in the ancient days, pre-social media. Prior to finding these friends, the only access I had to other mothers were occasional phone calls with women in my family or friends who lived in far-flung places. There are many obvious ways in which social media might exacerbate isolation, but I often think how different things would have felt back then had I such easy and open access to other new moms that online communities afford. Many women don't have access to a community like the one I eventually found. That online community exists is good and can be a bridge, a source of encouragement, advice, and connection. But it should never replace an opportunity to approach another new mom in a parking lot. If possible, community and conversation are always best in person, with all the messy, in-the-moment stutters and missteps, and the sound of each other's laughter.

Pineapples

When introduced to Europeans, the pineapple was some-what of a celebrity fruit due to its rarity and high demand. Closely associated with tropical environments, it was used as centerpieces or for gifts reserved for the most exclusive of recipients. Eventually, this translated into the exotic fruit becoming a cultural symbol of hospitality. A truly gracious host would lavish a guest with the very best, often conclud-ing a fine meal with sliced pineapple as dessert. Incorporation into finials, gateposts, and other architectural motifs solidified its reputation as a universal sign of welcome and hospitality.

CHAPTER 9

Harvest

One of the biggest struggles of homemaking is that it can feel like it matters very little in the grand scheme of things. Homemakers rarely have the sense that their daily activities of vacuuming, doing the dishes, kissing away pains, and guiding teenagers make much of an impact upon the world. But if we pull our perspective back, we can see the effects on a society which has devalued these efforts. Being home to meet children after school, spending time reading stories, tidying a well-lived-in house, preparing a special meal for a family birthday—these seemingly small things have a secret: they have the capacity to make tremendous ripples in the culture that, over time, spread out and echo into the future.

There is an old Spanish saying that says, "An ounce of mother is worth a pound of priests," which is not meant as a slight at all to the priesthood but a recognition that when the hard work of mothering is done right, it leads to lives of virtue that spread beyond themselves. In the book *Unwanted: How Sexual Brokenness Reveals Our Way to Healing,* author Jay Stringer discusses how many sexual struggles adults have because of the neglect they experienced as a child or adolescent. We have intrinsic human needs that, when not met, leave voids which are often filled by dangerous or disordered surrogates. What we do or don't do in the home matters not just in the home but spills over into the culture for better or for worse.

Susan Wingate

Susan is a mother of nine, grandmother of sixty-seven, and great-grandmother to three (with two more on the way). Affectionately called "Mumps," she is a woman who exudes a quiet joy, with a fire of faith and love burning behind her piercing blue eyes. She can pepper you with delightful stories that only a Southern woman could tell, but also offers uncommon wisdom and advice from her many years of life well-lived.

Yet the fire of joy wasn't always there. As a young woman experiencing the ups and downs of life with nine children, she was taught a profound lesson by her son, Christopher.

"He had a favorite song with this verse: 'This is the day the Lord has made, Let us rejoice and be glad in it.' He would always ask me to sing it and for a long time it was just a pleasant song."

Eventually, though, the song took on new meaning for Susan.

"Our Lord used it for a profound message. Like the biblical image of the paralytic man being lowered through the roof, this song that had been a pleasant message in my head was lowered into my heart, deep inside of me. I realized I could no longer give into my moodiness and emotions, which were often a roller coaster, but that it is much, much better to be rejoicing every day, no matter what is going on."

As a young woman, Susan had finished her coursework for a Master's degree in English literature. In an effort to help her complete her degree, her husband, Henry, a college librarian, arranged for her to have a carrel and a babysitter twice a

week so she could get her thesis written. But with three small children, their efforts were not very successful.

"I would walk there, sit down and read for a while, then put my head down and go to sleep. Henry's office was beneath my carrel, so at 5:00 p.m., he would hit his ceiling with a broom stick and wake me up. I'd get up, straighten up my things, and we'd walk home together. I don't remember writing anything."

Although she wishes she had finished the degree, it isn't something she misses. Having a large family has filled her in ways far more than any degree could, though having so many kids wasn't something she and Henry set out to do; it happened gradually, despite her own struggles and concerns about the demands of caring for another child or trying to lose weight in between births. Their family, Susan makes clear, has brought a richness to their life.

"Biblically, Our Lord tells us children are our inheritance, and that's how we feel about all of them. We think of an inheritance as such a blessing, and children are always that, never as a minus, always as a plus. My husband used to say, 'Children don't cost anything.'" What he meant, Susan explains, was that the expenses related to raising children aren't a burden but a blessing.

Even now, at a season of life when people are expected to spend their time golfing or traveling, Susan doesn't feel weighed down by her large family. Inspired by a video she saw of Elizabeth Elliot many years before she became a grandmother, Susan feels strongly that grandparents can support their children and grandchildren in many ways, guiding them and helping them develop their character.

"Our comfort, pleasure, and fun," Susan says, "come from the children."

With such a large family, one might wonder how Susan builds a bond with each of them.

"I feel like my part-time job is remembering their birthdays," she says with a chuckle. Uninterested in giving them just money, Susan says she looks at her calendar at the start of each month for the upcoming birthdays and figures out who might be interested in what. She then shops at thrift stores or used bookstores to find suitable gifts. "Finding the right thing for each one takes a lot of my time and effort, but is it a wonderful way of connecting with that child."

As for advice for young mothers, Susan offers one of her biggest lessons.

"For young mothers, as you go along, there the children are. All day. All night. They want your attention, and you are using every single thing you have got—your intellect, your body, your tenderness, your corrections: they are milking you for everything you have. Sometimes it is a very natural reaction (unless I'm the only selfish woman in the world) to just want to keep something for yourself. I wanted some quiet time, time to think my own thoughts. I finally learned that it is important to just surrender, to stop cleaning and give myself over to them. It always turned out to be the happiest part of the day. In raising children, it is important not to hold back something of yourself. That is where joy begins."

"The other thing I do, is I ask the Lord for wisdom every day, for myself but also for every member of my family. In James 1:5, the Lord promises that if we lack wisdom, he will give it to us. That is something I truly want all of them to have."

Restoring a Destroyed Cathedral

Dietrich von Hildebrand compared the work of a woman to the building of a great cathedral—that in the midst of such work we might be daunted, seeing only the dust and the demand, wary of the value of any individual day. It is tempting to undermine it, to think our lives are too important for such obscurity. The precursor to this is a loss of a sense of the eternal, which, once lost in desire, is inevitably lost in attainment.

It is striking how we can take for granted what has been built and established over centuries and yet feel its importance only as we watch its demise. Centuries of giving preeminence to family life, done however imperfectly and fallibly, is like a hidden monument whose power threatens to be known only in its disappearance. It is not something that we can let go without anything short of an earthquake.

"Each generation is converted by
the saint who contradicts it most."

– G. K. CHESTERTON –

I heard the news that Notre Dame Cathedral was on fire while en route to midday Mass. In an apparent coincidence, or a matter of providence, the Gospel reading for the day was the story of Judas criticizing Mary for lavishing costly oils onto Christ's feet. Judas objected that it was a gratuitous and wasteful act and represented money which could have gone to the poor. I always think of cathedrals when I hear this Gospel story—the deep devotion that inspired their lavish construction, and the devotion and conversion that they inspire in us.

Notre Dame was built over an almost two-hundred-year period. Generations of people came and went, investing their days in this life for the sake of a project, the fulfillment of which they knew they would not live to see.

The Feminine Role in Culture

Art historian Sir Kenneth Clark stated that there is something unusual about the feminine element in religion and culture. Sir Clark says, "The all-male religions (a reference to Israel, Islam, and the Protestant North) have produced no religious imagery—in most cases have positively forbidden it. The great religious art of the world is deeply involved in the female principle."

The Virgin Mary certainly offers that feminine principle. No woman has been more painted in all of human history. She has inspired countless artists, poets, philosophers, authors, architects, musicians, and theologians.

Mary's influence in these isn't art for art's sake, but like Mary herself, points to something, or in this case, *someone*, beyond herself. To see the material elements of Marian culture, such as art, music, architecture, and literature, the viewer doesn't simply bask in its beauty or cleverness for its own sake but, wittingly or not, enters into Christ's story.

Christ and the Church in their wisdom saw fit to give us a mother so we would not be left orphans. At the heart of every family is a mother. And it is from the mother that culture can and does flow—because she brings order, connection between members, a deep sense of belonging, and the safety that comes from just being known and held. Mary, as the perfect mother, fulfills this role. And in those times and places when she has been at the center of a culture—the true mother of the family—cultures have flourished.

It is difficult to wrap our minds around what a culture might look like where women emphasize fruit over power and control. Those with a skewed understanding of theology, human nature, and history have suggested it would resemble *The Handmaid's Tale*. But the manifestation of a Marian culture would look quite different, to say the least.

Without harkening back to an age we cannot recreate, we can see how minor changes in the way we think about ourselves can make subtle changes in our families—immediate and extended—but also in our places of work. Small things like listening more, being more tender, making fewer rash judgements, and figuring out the genuine needs of others. It may seem that we cannot change the world in which we live, but these small efforts of cultivating our own spiritual plot of land can have far reaching effects, planting seeds that can be sown today but also by future generations.

We have evidence of real harvesting in the maternal hearts of women like St. Monica, who prayed her son, Augustine, into the Church, which left an imprint on Christian theology that we still feel today; or St. Catherine, whose holiness was so well known she convinced the pope in Avignon to return to Rome; or the countless other female saints, known and unknown, who have shaped civilization with their prayers, tears, and efforts for those in their care.

Hours and days and money and energy were expended that could have been spent strictly focusing on other practical needs. In the cold calculation of a culture that has lost a sense of the eternal and of God himself, lavishly adoring Our Lord without an obvious worldly reward makes no sense.

"Gardens are not made by singing 'Oh, how
beautiful,' and sitting in the shade."

– RUDYARD KIPLING –

And yet, there we were, religious or not, watching this fire with dread and shock, and collectively feeling the trauma and magnitude of this potential loss, followed by relief when it turned out not to be total.

Our reverence for Notre Dame is certainly a reverence for its consummate majesty. It is also a reverence for those who built it, their patient devotion and our disquieting desire for the one who inspired it.

Seeing the French on their knees, clutching rosaries, and singing to Our Lady of both victory and sorrow, our Mother and our Queen, we have the sense of a seed of the old faith fighting to enliven our dormant hearts.

While the rapid devastation of a fire dramatically highlighted what we stood to lose, the slow dismantling of the family has been happening over the course of many decades. It is a dismantling that has left us stunted, wounded, and reactionary. To be immersed in the temporal is to miss a true perspective on the loss entirely. A culture accompanied by the legion of pathologies that are inevitable when we flatten our identities into a malleable misshapen mess is not healed by new gender theories, feminist literature, "be nice" campaigns, or corporate sermons on consent. Such efforts are trying to address a fire with caution tape.

But there is indeed a seed of the old faith fighting to take deeper root and grow, restoring the monumental force that is pure and ordered love. We witness to its magnitude with every harvest feast—from family dinners to

wedding feasts to our return again and again from our prodigal ways to the banquet at the holy sacrifice of the Mass. In delivering a powerful nuptial homily, a family friend, Fr. Joseph Illo, described beautifully the mission of the woman. "You will notice that the [nuptial] blessing focuses more on the woman than the man; some say it imposes a disproportionate responsibility on the woman. In one sense, women do bear the greater responsibility for marriage and family life, even as they have born each of us for nine months in their bodies and for life, in their hearts. 'The future of humanity passes by way of the family,' St. John Paul wrote in 1981, and I might add that the family itself passes through the heart of the mother. If Mamma's not happy, nobody's happy."

We have the capacity to reclaim this happiness in the heart of every woman. The answer, like most things in the Christian life, is not the obvious one—it is not in self-gratification, self-scrutiny, self-esteem. Trying to rebuild ourselves, our loved ones, and the culture through these means is like suggesting that the builders of Notre Dame scrutinize their skills and tools rather than getting to the hard work of hewing timbers and shingles. The answer is in turning our gaze to the other—first to God, then to our husbands, children, extended family, and neighbor. This clear answer, if not immediately obvious, is repeatedly impressed upon us throughout a lifetime. We don't become happy by being consumed with the achievement of our own happiness. Willing the good and working toward that end in the lives of others in a way that is not arid but ardent is the very footpath to happiness. In the small work of building a home, with tenderness and levity, attention and devotion, we become an expansive force in the rebuilding of society.

———————————

"We are a restless, mobile people,
but not really travelers.
We are wanderers.
We were meant, however,
to be pilgrims: people on pilgrimage
toward an ultimate destination,
our final home."

– FR. PAUL DONLAN –

———————————

Of the symbolism we have considered for women, the symbol of a ship might best encompass this great work. A ship has direction, a mission, a destination. It is on the move. A ship is also of considerable substance, literally weighing tens of thousands of tons. Yet it skims upon the surface of the water with apparent ease. A ship is a beautiful combination of formidable gravity, paired with baffling lightness. It is powerful, but power is not its point. Its power is merely to serve its greater purpose of reaching its destination, and getting those whom she carries with her there as well.

Grain and Grapes

Grain and grapes are the most essential fruits in the Christian tradition. Both are required for the Mass in the form of the bread and wine, which become the Body and Blood of Christ.

In John's Gospel, grains of wheat are a metaphor for the dying to self that we all must do to "[bear] much fruit" (Jn 12:24). Grapes must go through a similar process as they are pressed or stomped to release their juice that is transformed into wine. In both cases, the original product must be transformed into something new through a "painful" process, but when complete, it is much better than the original.

Curiously, bread made from wheat has a relatively short shelf-life and can't be stored indefinitely without preservatives. Wine, on the other hand, is on the opposite end of the agricultural spectrum. The process of growing grapes and wine making can't be done overnight; it takes time, care, the right weather conditions, and the wisdom of a vintner to get a bottle of wine just right. A well-made and hearty vintage can be stored for decades, while bread can dry up in just days. Even Noah must have known this, for after the ark "docked" on dry land, the first crop he planted was grape vines.

Wheat, because of John's Gospel, has come to symbolize rebirth and resurrection. In art, various depictions of it evoke different meanings. For example, wheat in a basket is a symbol of self-sacrifice, images of wheat being sown symbolizes penitence, and a man or woman harvesting it is symbolic of fertility or productivity.

Grapes in pagan art were a sign of abundant feasting, drunkenness, and debauchery, but in Christian art, because of the connection with the Eucharist, grapes are symbols of salvation, fertility, and truth.

Afterword

I remember after my first child was born how much more important water seemed—nursing brought a seemingly unquenchable thirst, and all the washing, wiping, and wringing that went along with newborn life was overwhelming. Even the key element of my daughter's initiation into the Church relied upon water. I felt a new appreciation for running hot water, showers, and all the speedy ways to heat water. I tried to imagine the daily effort it must have taken women to keep clothing, tiny bottoms, hands, and hair clean, particularly when they relied upon a well or spring as their only source of water. How good we have it.

Water is perhaps the most profound metaphor we have for God's grace and abundance. It is life-giving and purifying in a physical sense but also on the spiritual level. All of us yearn for it—although perhaps unwittingly—as we yearn for water when we are thirsty. Like the Samaritan woman at the well, we long for the water that will never leave us thirsting again. Drought, the desert, and aridity have long been symbols of God removing his favor from mankind, a sign that we must be stripped of our attachments so that we might cling more purely to him. In becoming aware of the depth of our spiritual poverty, we begin to thirst for God to pour his grace upon us, to restore and confirm the relationship we have with him. Out of this relationship, watered by grace and love, fruit grows, even in the midst of aridity or obstacles (and sometimes because of them).

Saints and Roses

Over the centuries, roses have come to have a prominent place in Christianity. The name of the rosary came from the offering of a garland of roses to Our Lady. In the apparition of Our Lady of Guadalupe, the miraculous roses hand-placed by Mary in St. Juan Diego's tilma fell to the ground and revealed the image of Our Lady on the tilma, an image that is still imprinted on it five hundred years later. St. Therese is known to confirm answered prayers by sending roses, and St. Elizabeth of Hungary is associated with carrying an apron full of roses.

St. Ambrose speculated that before the fall, roses did not have thorns, but after the fall, thorns developed to remind us of original sin. Our Lady, he says, is the rose without thorns because of her immaculate conception. More than a millennia later, St. John Henry Newman, when explaining Mary's title of Mystical Rose, wrote: "Mary is the queen of spiritual flowers, and therefore she is called the rose, for the rose is fitly called of all the flowers, the most beautiful. But moreover, she is the mystical or hidden rose, for mystical means hidden. Mary, born without original sin, is also without thorns and the scent is an emblem of her spirit."

Greenness

The only real source for fruitfulness is God. Though an ancient concept, St. Hildegard of Bingen (1098–1179) put her own unique stamp upon the idea of fruitfulness back in the twelfth century. St. Hildegard, a Benedictine nun and abbess, was an intellectual force for her age. Made a doctor of the Church by Pope Benedict XVI, she was a writer, composer, and philosopher. She was also a mystic who experienced visions from God.

One of the recurring concepts in her work is the idea of *viriditas*, or greenness. For St. Hildegard, this concept wasn't just an ecological principal as we might consider it today. *Viriditas* was tightly bound up with the notion that all greenness, all life, comes directly from the great and abundant greenness of God. Even this idea of a color for an abstract concept points to the vivid nature of St. Hildegard's visions and intellect. Although she uses it in many ways, most commonly she associates it with vitality, fertility, abundance, growth, and lushness. Greenness, St. Hildegard explains, is seen in creation's abundance. Both the earth and the soul require water (grace) to work with nature to bring about the flourishing of human nature. Greenness emanating from God's goodness provides the vitality necessary for life. Without it, there can be no physical or spiritual health. Greenness does not exist apart from God.

St. Hildegard uses the rich imagery of gardening and farming to emphasize that it is only God's gifts of sun and rain that bring out true fruit. As explained in the *Selected Writings* of St. Hildegard's work, a field can be sown by man, but divine power provides "the moisture of fresh greenness and the warmth of sunlight which cause the crop to bear fruit." Similarly, Hildegard explains, "a person can 'sow a word' in another's ear, but only God can send irrigation and bring forth the fruit of holiness."

While we are required to do our part in sowing seeds or words, our efforts are limited and can only be successful with God's provision. St. Hildegard, who was not ignorant of Scripture, echoes the book of Job, where God asks who provided the "rain on a land where no man is, . . . to satisfy the waste and desolate land, and to make the ground put forth grass?" (Job 38:26–27). No matter how focused, how thought out, or how well-intended our efforts might be, they will not be fertile unless accompanied by God's grace.

St. Faustina's Roses

St. Faustina's life was punctuated by poverty, pain, miracles, and mercy. As the emissary for the Divine Mercy Chaplet, this cloistered nun lived in "a thin place," as author Emily Stimpson Chapman would call it. It is a place where the veil between heaven and earth nearly touch and grace and mercy seem to weave back and forth easily between the two realms.

In her diary, the future saint chronicled one of these moments where the mundane gave way to the miraculous. One of the regular tasks in the cloistered kitchen was to drain the water off of a large pot of boiled potatoes. Given her frailty from illness, it was an arduous task that Sister Faustina tried to avoid. After taking it to Our Lord in prayer, he told her interiorly, "From today on, you will do this easily; I shall strengthen you."

Later that day, when it was time to drain the potatoes, Sister Faustina rushed to the task, trusting that she would be able to do it as Christ had promised. She poured out the water with ease. But then looking in the pot, she saw that what remained was not potatoes but red roses. The roses, she said, were beautiful beyond description. Confused by this dinner miracle, she asked for an explanation. She heard an interior voice say, "I change such hard work of yours into bouquets of the most beautiful flowers, and their perfume rises up to My throne."

This image and these words can stay with us all, thinning the veil in the demands of daily work.

Full Bloom

Flowers are something of a mystery in the world today with our tendency to focus on usefulness. Flowers grow but die quickly. While some fruit comes from them, mostly they seem to serve little purpose. Most can't be eaten or remade into something else aside from gathering seeds, or drying them. And yet we love them. A bouquet of flowers can draw the eye and bring beauty to a room. We offer them to those who are suffering, celebrating, and mourning. They communicate love, and a good beyond that of mere use in their seemingly frivolous abundance, even in their fleeting beauty.

"My garden is my most beautiful masterpiece."

– CLAUDE MONET –

In his work *Meditations and Devotions*, John Henry Newman described the spiritual significance of flowers and fruit as a sign of God's goodness. They "speak of His sanctity, His love, and His providence." St. John Newman reasons that if flowers and fruits are signs of these Godly gifts, so too must be the place where they are sowed, nurtured, and grown. "[A] garden has also excellences which speak of God, because it is their [fruits and flower's] home," he explains. This is why Eden is described as a garden, Christ's agony began in a garden, and heaven is compared to a lush garden. Gardens are a place where souls who have been cultivated by the Gardener manifest the beauty of his careful efforts. Flowers and fruits are mystically the gifts and graces of God and the "garden is meant mystically [to be] a place of spiritual repose, stillness, peace, refreshment, and delight."

The rich imagery of the gardener and his garden makes it easy to see that Mary is rightfully called the greatest flower among created beings. St. John Newman describes her as "the choice, delicate, perfect flower of God's spiritual creation." Mariologist Fr. Johann Roten calls Mary God's masterpiece.

"As *masterpiece*, Mary is a direct reference to the divine *artifex*: she is part of the creative manifestation of God's marvelous deeds." He continues, "Mary's beauty is beauty of promise and hope."

"Gratitude and love increase each other; joy is their blessed fruit."

– FRIEDERIKE GÖRRES –

As Christians, we are offered participation in the life of the divine Artist by the lives we live and those we carry, shelter, nourish, and love. By her model as our mother and queen, Mary both embodies and points us to what is true, good, and beautiful, emboldening us to bear good fruit no matter what our unique call might be. The challenge for the Christian is to see with a vision that encompasses the scope of this grand history, along with this window into the eternal, and bring both into our present everyday lives.

The Garden's Order

For years I wanted a garden and to share the experience of cultivating it with my kids. But our soil was too rocky to just start planting, so raised beds were necessary. I had a carpenter build them and soil was delivered. Seeds had been selected and we were finally ready to plant. Standing over all that potential, I realized I didn't know what to do. It was a similar feeling to the day my firstborn was handed to me to nurse. Nursing always looked so simple on TV, but I immediately realized that I didn't know the first thing about nursing a child. Gratefully, the nursing consultant helped me through those first early days. But what I needed now was a gardening consultant. Gratefully, I found one in the largely self-taught homeschooler with a green thumb who got us through the first few days.

After trips to the nursery for various odds and ends, we were ready to just sit back and watch our garden grow. And grow it did! One of the planters was full of squash. Each morning, I would look out my bedroom window to see the progress. I marveled at the size of the leaves and the beauty of the squash flowers. For weeks, it was a joy to wake up and see them in full bloom, only to close up tightly as the day heated up. They were bursting with life and energy, stretching slowly but resolutely out of the ground. And then the fruit began to grow snuggly under the leaves. As the squash grew, the flowers dropped and the leaves started to wane, as if saying, "Our work is done here. We have passed along the seeds necessary for the next plant to grow." And they faded like a sunset.

All of this struck a sharp chord with me as I carried a child "under my own heart," as they used to say. I felt a new interest in the vibrant orange flowers, recognizing the gift of youth, energy, and beauty they represented. But I felt more sympathy for the

waning plant, having offered every bit of its own life to secure future life. At forty-six, I felt more like a completely exhausted plant than a glowing young woman in "full bloom." And yet, the garden offered visual consolation of the divine order sown into creation from the start of seed, flower, fruit, and death. Gardeners and farmers know this deep in their souls as they cooperate with this order from season to season. A return to the soil is a reminder that our lives happen not just for us but for the sake of the future, that we are always called to pay it forward, that we are always called to bear fruit.

Acknowledgments

A book like this requires a lot of help from others. We are so grateful to all those who helped us with this project, particularly as we all lived through the throes of the 2020 coronavirus quarantine. We couldn't have done it without the many people who assisted us in getting this book done on time.

Special thanks to those who opened their homes up to us: Blythe and Kirby Fike, Brooke Collins, Paul and Leigha Doerrer, DeNai and Braden Jones, Sue Wise, Susan Wingate, Anne Sheely, Hazel Baile, Jenna Wilber, Daniel Wilber, Julia Marsh, Wes and Amina Bancroft, Jessica Haggard, Korie and Will Conant, Danny and Meg Bowman.

We are grateful to those whose stories and influence were sprinkled throughout.

There were also so many who helped us with input on the substance of the book or behind the scenes to make sure everything looked perfect. Thanks to Fr. Paul Donlan, Andrew Whaley, Flora Lee Design, Susanna and Elizabeth Wise, Patrick Bereit, and Bethany Wingate, Hope Schneir, Nicole Tittmann, Amy Dragoo, Theresa Dillon, Jessica Haggard, Joseph and Helen Thompson, Mary Curphey, Maarja Miley, Rochelle Storts, Mary Peterson, Jenny Lee, Christina Marotti, and Calise Green.

We would especially like to thank the women who shared their personal stories with us: Leigha Doerrer, Susan Wingate, Kathleen Wilson, Blythe Fike,

Fike, Brooke Collins, Muji Kaiser, Jennifer Bryson, Josefina Boles, and Lucia Zinkewich.

We continue to be grateful for the hard work of our colleagues at TAN Books, including Brian Kennelly, Caroline Green, Chris Cona, Zack Flannick, Sara Maldonado, Paul Grabowski, Nick Vari, Katie DeMoss, Mara Persic, and Robert and Conor Gallagher.

Special thanks to the cloistered Norbertine Canonesses of Tehachapi, California, for their friendship, prayers, and for allowing us to use images of their beautiful community.

And perhaps most significantly, we would like to thank our families for their patience, assistance, inspiration, and hard work in helping us to see this project to the finish, especially our amazing husbands, Mark, Joseph, and Adam.

Thank you also to the publications that allowed us to use excerpts from our articles in this project.

Bibliography

"Why Women Love the Home, But Not Being a Homemaker," *The Federalist*, Sept. 26, 2019.

"The Subtle Lie that Women Must Be Powerful But Not Fruitful," *Catholic World Report*, July 7, 2019.

"Finding Home Amid Ruptured Relationships," *National Review*, Aug. 17, 2019.

"Women: To Work or Not to Work," Catholic World Report, Oct. 22, 2019.

"Our Lady and the Snow," *Catholic World Report*, Jan. 23, 2016.

St. John Henry Newman, *Meditations and Devotions*, Newmanreader.com.

"It Is All Who You Know," *National Catholic Register*, Jan. 11, 2016.

St. Hildegard of Bingen, *Selected Works*, Penguin Classics, Trans. by Mark Atherton, Kindle Edition.

G. K. Chesterton, *The Collected Works of G. K. Chesterton*, vol. 2 (San Francisco: Ignatius Press, 1987).